15 Days of Prayer
With Saint Francis de Sales

Also in the *15 Days of Prayer* collection:

15 DAYS OF PRAYER

WITH

Saint Francis de Sales

CLAUDE MOREL

Translated by Victoria Hébert and Denis Sabourin

Liguori
LIGUORI, MISSOURI

Published by Liguori Publications
Liguori, Missouri
http://www.liguori.org

This book is a translation of *Prier 15 Jours Avec François de Sales*,
published by Nouvelle Cité, 1994, Montrouge, France.

English Translation Copyright 2000 by Liguori Publications.

Library of Congress Cataloging-in-Publication Data

Claude Morel
[Prier 15 jours avec François. English]
15 days of prayer with Saint Francis de Sales / Claude Morel ; trans-
lator, Victoria Hébert and Denis Sabourin. — 1st English ed.
p. cm.
ISBN 0-7648-0575-4 (pbk)
1. Francis, de Sales, Saint, 1567–1622—Prayer-books and devotions—
English. I. Title: Fifteen days of prayer with Saint Francis de Sales. II.
Title.
BX2179.F63 M6713 2000
269'.6—dc21   99-046203

Printed in the United States of America
04 03 02 01 00   5 4 3 2 1
First English Edition 2000

Table of Contents

How to Use This Book

AN OLD CHINESE PROVERB, or at least what I am able to recall of what is supposed to be an old Chinese proverb, goes something like this: "Even a journey of a thousand miles begins with a single step." When you think about it, the truth of the proverb is obvious. It is impossible to begin any project, let alone a journey, without taking the first step. I think it might also be true, although I cannot recall if another Chinese proverb says it, "that the first step is often the hardest." Or, as someone else once observed, "the distance between a thought and the corresponding action needed to implement the idea takes the most energy." I don't know who shared that perception with me but I am certain it was not an old Chinese master!

With this ancient proverbial wisdom, and the not-so-ancient wisdom of an unknown contemporary sage still fresh, we move from proverbs to presumptions. How do these relate to the task before us?

I am presuming that if you are reading this introduction it is because you are contemplating a journey. My presumption is that you are preparing for a spiritual journey and that you have taken at least some of the first steps necessary to prepare for this journey. I also presume, and please excuse me if I am making too many presumptions, that in your preparation for the spiritual journey you have determined that you need a guide. From deep within the recesses of your deepest self, there was something that called you to consider Francis de Sales as a potential companion. If my presumptions are correct, may I congratulate you on this decision? I think you have made a wise choice, a choice that can be confirmed by yet another source of wisdom, the wisdom that comes from practical experience.

Even an informal poll of experienced travelers will reveal a common opinion; it is very difficult to travel alone. Some might observe that it is even foolish. Still others may be even stronger in their opinion and go so far as to insist that it is necessary to have a guide, especially when you are traveling into uncharted waters and into territory that you have not yet experienced. I am of the personal opinion that a traveling companion is welcome under all circumstances. The thought of traveling alone, to some exciting destination without someone to share the journey with does not capture my imagination or channel my enthusiasm. However, with that being noted, what is simply a matter of preference on the normal journey becomes a matter of necessity when a person embarks on a spiritual journey.

The spiritual journey, which can be the most challenging of all journeys, is experienced best with a guide, a companion, or at the very least, a friend in whom you have placed your trust. This observation is not a preference or an opinion but rather an established spiritual necessity. All of the great saints with whom I am familiar had a spiritual director or a confessor who journeyed with them. Admittedly, at times the saint might well have traveled far beyond the experience of their guide and companion but more often than not they would return to their director and reflect on their experience. Understood in this sense, the director and companion provided a valuable contribution and necessary resource.

When I was learning how to pray (a necessity for anyone who desires to be a full-time and public "religious person"), the community of men that I belong to gave me a great gift. Between my second and third year in college, I was given a one-year sabbatical, with all expenses paid and all of my personal needs met. This period of time was called novitiate. I was officially designated as a novice, a beginner in the spiritual journey, and I was assigned a "master," a person who was willing to lead me. In addition to the master, I was provided with every imaginable book and any other resource that I could possibly need. Even with all that I was provided, I did not learn how to pray because of the books and the unlimited resources; rather it was the master, the companion who was the key to the experience.

One day, after about three months of reading, of quiet and solitude, and of practicing all of the methods and descriptions of prayer that were available to me, the master called. "Put away the books, forget the method, and just listen." We went into a room, became quiet, and tried to recall the presence of God, and then, the master simply prayed out loud and permitted me to listen to his prayer. As he prayed, he revealed his hopes, his dreams, his struggles, his successes, and most of all, his relationship with God. I discovered as I listened that his prayer was deeply intimate but most of all it was self-revealing. As I learned about him, I was led through his life experience to the place where God dwells. At that moment I was able to understand a little bit about what I was supposed to do if I really wanted to pray.

The dynamic of what happened when the master called, invited me to listen, and then revealed his innermost self to me as he communicated with God in prayer, was important. It wasn't so much that the master was trying to reveal to me what needed to be said; he was not inviting me to pray with the same words that he used, but rather that he was trying to bring me to that place within myself where prayer becomes possible. That place, a place of intimacy and of self-awareness, was a necessary stop on the journey and it was a place that I needed to be led to. I could not have easily discovered it on my own.

The purpose of the volume that you hold in your hand is to lead you, over a period of fifteen days or, maybe more realistically, fifteen prayer periods, to a place where prayer is possible. If you already have a regular experience and practice of prayer, perhaps this volume can help lead you to a deeper place, a more intimate relationship with the Lord.

It is important to note that the purpose of this book is not to lead you to a better relationship with Francis de Sales, your spiritual companion. Although your companion will invite you to share some of their deepest and most intimate thoughts, your companion is doing so only to bring you to that place where God dwells. After all, the true measurement of a companion for the journey is that they bring you to the place where you need to be, and then they step back, out of the picture. A guide who brings you to the desired destination and then sticks around is a very unwelcome guest!

Many times I have found myself attracted to a particular idea or method for accomplishing a task, only to discover that what seemed to be inviting and helpful possessed too many details. All of my energy went to the mastery of the details and I soon lost my enthusiasm. In each instance, the book that seemed so promising ended up on my bookshelf, gathering dust. I can assure you, it is not our intention that this book end up in your bookcase, filled with promise, but unable to deliver.

There are three simple rules that need to be followed in order to use this book with a measure of satisfaction.

Place: It is important that you choose a place for reading that provides the necessary atmosphere for reflection and that does not allow for too many distractions. Whatever place you choose needs to be comfortable, have the necessary lighting, and, finally, have a sense of "welcoming" about it. You need to be able to look forward to the experience of the journey. Don't travel steerage if you know you will be more comfortable in first class and if the choice is realistic for you. On the other hand, if first class is a distraction and you feel more comfortable and more yourself in steerage, then it is in steerage that you belong.

My favorite place is an overstuffed and comfortable chair in my bedroom. There is a light over my shoulder, and the chair reclines if I feel a need to recline. Once in a while, I get lucky and the sun comes through my window and bathes the entire room in light. I have other options and other places that are available to me but this is the place that I prefer.

Time: Choose a time during the day when you are most alert and when you are most receptive to reflection, meditation, and prayer. The time that you choose is an essential component. If you are a morning person, for example, you should choose a time that is in the morning. If you are more alert in the afternoon, choose an afternoon time slot; and if evening is your preference, then by all means choose the evening. Try to avoid "peak" periods in your daily routine when you know that you might be disturbed. The time that you choose needs to be your time and needs to work for you.

It is also important that you choose how much time you will spend with your companion each day. For some it will be possible to set aside enough time in order to read and reflect on all the material that is offered for a given day. For others, it might not be possible to devote one time to the suggested material for the day, so the prayer period may need to be extended for two, three, or even more sessions. It is not important how long it takes you; it is only important that it works for you and that you remain committed to that which is possible.

For myself I have found that fifteen minutes in the early morning, while I am still in my robe and pajamas and before my morning coffee, and even before I prepare myself for the day, is the best time. No one expects to see me or to interact with me because I have not yet "announced" the fact that I am awake or even on the move. However, once someone hears me in the bathroom, then my window of opportunity is gone. It is therefore important to me that I use the time that I have identified when it is available to me.

Freedom: It may seem strange to suggest that freedom is the third necessary ingredient, but I have discovered that it is most important. By freedom I understand a certain "stance toward life," a "permission to be myself and to be gentle and understanding of who I am." I am constantly amazed at how the human person so easily sets himself or herself up for disappointment and perceived failure. We so easily make judgments about ourselves and our actions and our choices, and very often those judgments are negative, and not at all helpful.

For instance, what does it really matter if I have chosen a place and a time, and I have missed both the place and the time for three days in a row? What does it matter if I have chosen, in that twilight time before I am completely awake and still a little sleepy, to roll over and to sleep for fifteen minutes more? Does it mean that I am not serious about the journey, that I really don't want to pray, that I am just fooling myself when I say that my prayer time is important to me? Perhaps, but I prefer to believe that it simply means that I am tired and I just wanted a little more sleep. It doesn't mean anything more than that. However, if I make it mean more than that, then I can become discouraged, frustrated, and put myself into a state where I might more easily give up. "What's the use? I might as well forget all about it."

The same sense of freedom applies to the reading and the praying of this text. If I do not find the introduction to each day helpful, I don't need to read it. If I find the questions for reflection at the end of the appointed day repetitive, then I should choose to close the book and go my own way. Even if I discover that the reflection offered for the day is not the one that I prefer and that the one for the next day seems more inviting, then by all means, go on to the one for the next day.

That's it! If you apply these simple rules to your journey you should receive the maximum benefit and you will soon find yourself at your destination. But be prepared to be surprised. If you have never been on a spiritual journey you should know that the "travel brochures" and the other descriptions that you might have heard are nothing compared to the real thing. There is so much more than you can imagine.

A final prayer of blessing suggests itself:

Lord, catch me off guard today.
Surprise me with some moment of beauty
    or pain
So that at least for the moment
I may be startled into seeing that you are
    here in all your splendor,
Always and everywhere,
Barely hidden,
Beneath,
Beyond,
Within this life I breathe.

Frederick Buechner

REV. THOMAS M. SANTA, CSsR
LIGUORI, MISSOURI
FEAST OF THE PRESENTATION, 1999

A Brief Chronology of the Life of Saint Francis de Sales

1567: Francis de Sales was born on August 21, in Thorens (France); the eldest of a family of thirteen; both parents were of the nobility, having led exemplary Christian lives.

1574–1581:

Francis went to school in La Roche, a short distance from home; he left after two years to attend school in Annecy in an institution run by the secular clergy; on December 17, 1577, Francis received both his first Communion and confirmation; nine months later, on September 20, 1578, he was tonsured; he was already aware of his future vocation at this time in spite of his father's wishes that he enter the military. He was so determined to become a priest that he imposed upon himself the obligation to attend Mass on the first Sunday of every month (an unusual practice at the time).

1582–1587:

Francis left Annecy to attend the University of Paris at the Jesuit College in Clermont; he became a learned man, earning a bachelor's degree in arts, also studying theology and Scripture; spiritually, his life centered on meditation, devotion to the Eucharist and Mary, the recitation of the breviary and a promise to God of virginity.

1588–1590:

Francis returned to Annecy; his father wanted him to become a lawyer and a member of the Senate because of his extreme intelligence; Francis went to the University of Padua to study law but also studied theology, placing himself under the spiritual direction of the Jesuit, Anthony Possevin; Francis renewed his promise of virginity, drawing up a rule for his interior and exterior life and recited the Divine Office.

1591: Francis received his doctorate in both civil and canon law. His father suggested that Francis marry in spite of his desire to be a clergyman; he went to a cousin who secured an apostolic bull which conferred on Francis a position of dignity, provost of the Church of St. Peter in Geneva.

1593–1601:

Francis was ordained a priest on December 18; he volunteered a year later, in response to a request by the Duke of Savoy, to go to Chablais to renew the faith of that region, previously conquered by the Protestants; his missionary work began in September, 1594, passing from village to village with other priests, preaching, visiting Catholic families, and seeking converts; this had limited success, so Francis adopted a new tactic: he began writing and distributing short articles about doctrines of faith, written simply and in a straight-forward manner, criticizing the teachings of the reformers; this practice continued for two years, at the end of which, these articles were published. Francis had a special way with the people who were very receptive to him and the Church, he often engaged in public debates with the Calvinist ministers; his very successful stay here was to last for four years, culminating in the founding of a school under the Jesuits.

1602: Francis was instrumental in establishing a group of secular priests in Thonon, who followed the Oratorian rule to combat the reformers; he enjoyed great success, converting most of the inhabitants of the area.

Francis was consecrated a bishop on December 8 to the see of Geneva; he held diocesan synods; during one of these synods, the Roman rite for the administration of the sacraments was adopted; he taught his priests how to hear confessions; he conducted pre-ordination examinations of potential candidates for the priesthood; he had Catechism taught to the laity every Sunday and holy day; a confraternity was formed specifically for this purpose.

1604–1621:

Francis met a young widow, the Baroness Jeanne de Chantal, with whom he founded, three years later, the Order of the Visitation; their religious vows would take them to practice the virtues exemplified by Mary in her visit to Elizabeth—humility, piety, and mutual charity—and perform works of mercy for the poor and the sick; their first convent was established in 1610, with Madame de Chantal as cofounder and superioress; the rule changed and they became a cloistered order; twelve other monasteries were founded and the order, the Visitation of Holy Mary, was elevated to the dignity of a religious order in 1618.

During the years of his episcopate, Francis was a tireless writer, his writing comprised some twenty-six volumes. He preached more than 4000 sermons. His friends called him a preacher with charm and power, speaking as both a father and a teacher. He spoke in clear and simple language, wanting to draw hearts to God by love and gentleness. Two works which were published in his lifetime, "Introduction to the Devout Life" (1608) and "On the Love of God" (1616), are considered masterpieces in spiritual literature and classics. The former was written especially for those who live in the world and must seek sanctity; the latter, as a means to help those who were already consolidated in the will to seek perfection and wished to progress to their destiny, in close connection with Madame de Chantal and the Visitation. It is considered a history of his own love for God.

1622: On December 27, Francis was stricken with a cerebral hemorrhage and died the following day at the monastery of the Visitation in Lyon after giving his last word to a religious sister: "humility." He was beatified in 1661; canonized in 1665, and in 1877 was proclaimed a Doctor of the Church by Pope Pius IX. Various religious congregations were founded under his patronage: the Missionaries of St. Francis de Sales; the Oblates of St. Francis de Sales, the Salesians of Don Bosco; and the Sisters of St. Joseph.

He believed that the key to love of God was prayer. For busy people, he recommended that they retire at various times during the day to talk to God, and the ultimate test of prayer was a person's actions. He believed that the worst sin was to judge someone and gossip about them, for even if one says it in a loving way, they are doing it to look better themselves. People should be as gentle and forgiving with themselves as they should be with others.

Introduction

TO PRAY FOR 15 DAYS with Saint Francis de Sales is to allow oneself to be led towards God and one's neighbor by a marvelous man whose sanctity is alluring and demanding.

The only way for spiritual progress is through an opening to the Holy Spirit. It is he who sanctifies us, it is he who makes us understand the Father's loving plan, realized in Jesus Christ, the Savior. "For God so loved the world that he gave his only Son, so that everyone who believes in him may not perish but may have eternal life" (Jn 3:16).

Saint Francis de Sales' firm conviction was that God was the God of the human heart. If it is true that progressing in faith entails walking in a certain obscurity without seeing God, it is also true that God is with us and reveals his love to us. Our vocation is to be loved by God, who offers us to be his children; and it is also to respond to this love. This is possible only through the prolongation of knowledge, through the prolongation of a better understanding of the single essential to life: God is love. All of Francis de Sales' teachings are to assist us in this progression to sanctity by helping us advance in the contemplation of God's marvels, beginning with the creation, providence, and the salvation, realized by Jesus Christ who died and rose from the dead.

To make a retreat with Saint Francis de Sales, to pray with

him under his direction, is to then renew our outlook on the grandeur of God and his goodness to us. A Doctor of God's love, he exhorts us to contemplate the one who is invisible, but who rendered himself visible through Jesus Christ. His purpose is to make us advance in an intimate relationship with God and to always live in his presence. Such a purpose remains current in a world that tends to lower our horizons to our interests which often seem to be very materialistic.

The intimate relationship that God offers us does not mean a love that is solely affective, it must be more than that, it must be effective. To live in the presence of God transforms our existence, and the love makes us want to do the will of God. Our outlook on daily realities is transformed. It becomes an outlook of happiness and trust for the people around us and for the events which occur. It is an outlook of faith which sees God in everything, placing everything in his love. "Since God loved us so much, we also ought to love one another" (1 Jn 4:11). The love for our neighbor is inseparable from the love for God; through faith, we must recognize God in the person of our brothers and sisters.

Untiringly, we must contemplate Christ, who lived in an intimate relationship with the Father, who did the Father's will and who offered himself totally to the Father by giving his life for us. To contemplate him is to imitate him and follow in his footsteps. Christ the Savior must be the heart of our lives; through his "holy Sacrifice of the Mass; our most holy, sacred and profound Sacrament and Sacrifice, the center of our faith, the heart of our devotion and the very soul of piety, the mystery in which God really communicates himself and gloriously showers his graces and favors on us."[1]

If we truly seek to conform ourselves to Christ, the Holy Spirit calls us to an always greater generosity. His presence in our lives always puts into question our relationships with others. Christians live in humility and happiness. They are free people who win this freedom by battling against egoism which tends to wear it down. By constantly seeking faithfulness, its soul become the soul of a poor person.

By calling us to sanctity, God gathers us together. He calls all of us in a personal way; but he wants us all to be members of his people, his Church. He mobilizes us all to build his kingdom and transmit the good news of the salvation of Jesus Christ to the world.

For each of us, the road to sanctity is a difficult one, because self-love and egoism are its faithful companions, they only die when we die. Only the Virgin Mary did not know the obstacle of sin. She is a model for the most beautiful sanctity. She is the one who knew how to contemplate God's marvels, the one who fulfilled the will of God through her generosity to the very end, the one who was the participant in the salvation of the world. She was also the one who manifested just how far the love of God can go by when we let ourselves be led by his Spirit of love: "for the Mighty One has done great things for me, and holy is his name" (Lk 1:49).

15 Days of Prayer
With Saint Francis de Sales

DAY ONE

The Grandeur of God

FOCUS POINT

There is an ineffable perfection to God. Our greatest enjoyment in life can come from simply being in God's loving presence. There have been many words written and spoken about God, describing him, hoping in some way to capture his grandeur. These attempts pale in comparison to the simplicity of just being "present" to God, sitting silently in his love.

"...In God there is neither variety nor difference whatsoever of perfection. He himself is absolutely one single most simple and most uniquely unique perfection. All that is in him is simply himself. All the excellences we say are in him in such great diversity are there in a most simple and most pure unity."[1]

We are called to holiness in our very own world, far removed from a sense of nostalgia for the past which no longer exists and faithful to the gospel which is forever. Our present era validates man's greatness and the strength of his intelligence as a result of his scientific discoveries which have led to technological advances and the sense of well being that has resulted from the evolution of technology. The result is evident: the greatness and strength of God is thrown into the shadows. The Church finds itself confronted with the problems of atheism and religious indifference.

THE MYSTERY OF GOD

So that our faith will be more radiant, let us contemplate on the mystery of God. Let ourselves be dazzled by his grandeur and splendor. Saint Francis de Sales proposes a comparison to us: the sun whose appearance and colors change throughout the day as well as throughout the seasons as a function of the state of the sky; grey, cloudy or clear. In reality, the sun does not have this variety of color, "but one clear single perpetual light which is above and beyond all color and that never changes."[2] It is the same with God: "we give him different names, as though he possessed a great number of different excellences and perfections. If we consider him as punishing the wicked, we call him just; if it is as delivering the sinner from misery, we proclaim him merciful. Since he has created all things and has performed many wonders, we call him all-powerful. In as much as he fulfills exactly what he has promised, we proclaim him true. In as much as he puts all things in such good order, we call him all-wise. In this manner, consecutively according to the great variety of his works, we attribute to him many different perfections. Nevertheless, in God there is neither variety nor any difference whatsoever of perfection. He himself is absolutely one, single, most simple, and uniquely unique perfection."[3]

ADORATION

Our intellect is truly incapable of grasping the totality of this unique and infinite perfection of God. We are faced with an unfathomable mystery which calls us to adoration: "let every spirit praise the Lord, calling him by the highest names that we can find. To render him the greatest praise within our power, let us confess that he can never be sufficiently praised."[4] Each time we say the Our Father, we proclaim: "hallowed be your name." We proclaim God's grandeur and we put ourselves before God, just as we are, in our smallness, in all confidence.

Adoration asks even more of us. The point is not to recognize the grandeur of a God that would be lost in the clouds; the point is to proclaim his presence acting in the world, to admit his sovereignty on earth like it is in heaven. The point is that God is the creator, not only of one single creation that would be a work that was accomplished once at the beginning of time that was for all time. He is the creator of today, tomorrow, and for all eternity.

There is a great temptation to misunderstand this creative action of God which continues with time. We all know that there are numerous people who are prisoners of a vision of the world that is strictly materialistic. If researchers always aim to better grasp how the world is constituted and to better understand the laws which regulate it, it is useless to explain the "whys" of things. For those who state that they are atheists, God is totally removed from their existence, he has no place in their explanation of the material world. However, "if man exists, it is God who has created him through love and, through love, he never stops giving him existence."⁵ It is true for man and for all of the universe, they are the fruit of the love of God the creator.

When we proclaim our faith and we say the Credo, we affirm that God is the creator of the world, both the visible and the invisible world. But does it mean that our approach to the mystery respects the truth? Are we not subject to another temptation, the one to see the work of creation unfurled in a multitude of varied and different actions, by casting aspersions on the very simple, unique, and infinite perfection of God? In a similar situation, would we not become "puppets," manipulated from above, incapable of doing anything for ourselves? We will always have difficulty in reconciling his all-powerfulness with our freedom and with the capacity that he has given us to work in a created world and transform it. It will always be impossible for us to understand the infinite meaning and simplicity of God.

Along with Saint Francis de Sales, let us again contemplate on this mystery of God; the comparison that he offers is fascinating. At his easel, the artist paints his masterpiece using thousands of brush strokes. It takes hour after hour of intensive work, and thousands of touch-ups before his painting appears in the manner and composition he desires so that the resulting creation best expresses his feelings as an artist. But if this work is reproduced by a printer, a single pass of the press is all that is necessary. It is the same with God: "But God, like the printer, has given existence to all the different creatures which have been, are, or shall be, by one single stroke of his all-powerful will. From his idea, as from a well-cut plate, he draws this marvelous distinction of persons and other things that succeed one another in seasons, ages, and times, each one in its order as they were destined to be."⁶

DIVINE PROVIDENCE

The material world is neither the result of chance, nor of necessity. It is the work of God who wanted it, with a sense of order and harmony that would favor his creature, man, made in his image and likeness. He governs and regulates this natural world according to his providence so that we will blossom. "Since God wills to provide men with the natural means necessary for them to render glory to his divine goodness, he has produced in their behalf all other animals and the plants, and to provide for the other animals and the plants, he has produced a variety of lands, seasons, waters, winds, and rains. Both for man and for those other things which belong to him, he created the elements, the sky, and the stars, ordaining in a wonderful way that practically all creatures should serve one another. Horses carry us, and we care for them. Sheep provide us with food and clothing, and we feed them. The earth sends vapors up into the air, and the air sends rain down upon the earth. The hand serves the foot, and the foot the hand."[7]

In its simplicity, this return to nature is an invitation to rediscover the work of God. He created us without having the need for us but to exercise his goodness. Before even manifesting itself through the grace and the glory that he proposes to us, his goodness first expresses itself in the creation and, amongst others, through the wealth of our human nature. God has given you "understanding to know him, memory to be mindful of him, free will to love him, imagination to picture for yourself his benefits, eyes to enjoy his creation, tongue and voice to praise him, and so with all the other faculties."[8]

Saint Augustine liked to say: "You made us for yourself, Lord, and our heart will never rest as long as it doesn't dwell with you." We live in a world which often misunderstands this grandiose work of creation. More and more our modern society is preoccupied with negative consequences which result from the scientific and technologic power of man. Society will realize that our environment is threatened only when the pollution of the air, rivers, lakes, and oceans and when the dangers of nuclear energy, the least of which being the overabundance of radioactive waste and the question of its disposal, risks compromising our own homes.

It is fundamental to be aware of the increase in the dangers which threaten us. It is even more fundamental to rediscover God's plan, etched in his work of creation, and grasp the order of things that he has placed here for us so that we could blossom there like his creatures.

REFLECTION QUESTIONS

In how many different ways do I recognize God's grandeur in my life? Do I see God's presence in nature, in the lives of those people around me, and in my own life? When I recognize his presence, do I run to meet God in those places, with my heart and mind ready for adoration and love?

DAY TWO

Brothers and Sisters in Jesus Christ

FOCUS POINT

Before salvation in Jesus Christ, we were brothers and sisters in sin, divided against each other in our relationships, just as our relationship with God was broken by the original sin of Adam. But now that we are saved, we are brothers and sisters unified in the saving grace of God, unified in one Mystical Body as brothers and sisters, just as we are unified with God.

"...From all eternity there is in God an essential communication by which the Father, in producing the Son, communicates his entire infinite and invisible divinity to the Son. The Father and the Son together, in producing the Holy Spirit, communicate in like manner their own proper unique divinity to him. So also this sovereign sweetness was communicated so per-

fectly outside itself to a creature that the created nature and the godhead each retained its own properties while still being united together in such ways that they were only one self-same person."[1]

T he context of our modern world reinforces the desire for autonomy which is etched in man's heart and worsened by sin to such a point that this desire for autonomy at times, becomes an obstacle to all dependence with regard to God. It is necessary for us to resituate ourselves before God and deepen our vocation. "The most sublime aspect of human dignity is found in this vocation of man communing with God. This invitation that God sends to man to enter into a dialogue with him begins at the time of human existence. Because, if man exists, it was God who created him through love and, through love, he never stops giving him his existence; and man will fully live according to the truth he recognizes only if he recognizes this love and abandons himself to his Creator."[2]

THE PROTOTYPE OF OUR HUMAN NATURE

What a marvel it is to see how Saint Francis de Sales underlines this intimate connection which exists between man and his Creator! To him, the first way of communicating his love had been for God to want Christ to have a human nature. The Lord's humanity is truly the prototype. Even if this prototype had only been realized later, when the Incarnate Word came into our history, it is the model the Creator wanted for us: "From eternity God knew that he would make an innumerable throng of creatures with different perfections and qualities and that he would communicate himself to them. He saw that among all different ways of communicating himself there was none so excellent as that of joining himself to a created nature in such ways that the creature would be engrafted and implanted in the godhead so as to become with it one single person...his infinite goodness...resolved and determined to affect a communication of this kind."[3]

Before even expressing the benevolence of God with regard to man as a sinner, the Incarnation of the Son of God manifested the divine will of communicating through love.

And in his love: "Supreme Providence then decreed that he would not restrict his bounty solely to the person of his beloved Son, but for that Son's sake he would diffuse it among many other creatures."[4] In this way, then, we have been created in the image and likeness of God, given that God gave us the gift of intelligence, desire, and the freedom to welcome his love and to respond to it through our own love. But we have also been created in the image and likeness of Christ, given that our humanity is a sort of reproduction of his own. Before becoming our savior and redeemer, Christ was our brother in humanity. Just like the Father wanted humanity for his Son, he wants our own; and we can repeat what the Psalmist said: "For it was you who formed my inward parts; you knit me together in my mother's womb" (Ps 139:13).

We must meditate on the story of man's creation from the Book of Genesis: "then the Lord God formed man from the dust of the ground, and breathed into his nostrils the breath of life; and the man became a living being" (Gen 2:7). This image which depicts God as a potter comes from the experience of death. The person who dies exhales a last breath (a final sigh); his body takes on a cadaver-like rigidity before experiencing corruption and returns to the earth. By taking us back, in an inverse order, through the events, the biblical author brings us to the essential idea: God is the source of our existence. Because he took us out of the humus of the ground, we must place ourselves in humility, literally, close to the ground. We must be conscious of our condition as a creature and recognize the sovereign domain of God over us. Faced with the infinite nature of God, the master of heaven and earth, we must recognize our radical powerlessness and finite nature.

MARKED BY SIN

At the root of sin is our refusal of our condition as creatures. What was the suggestion made to Adam and Eve by the tempter in the Garden of Eden? Faced with the prohibition of eating the fruit from the tree in the middle of the garden, "the serpent said to the woman, 'You will not die; for God knows that when you eat of it your eyes will be opened, and you will be like God, knowing good and evil'"(Gen 3:4–5).

That was the refusal to situate ourselves in truth. That was the search for fulfillment outside of God which proves to be impossible to achieve away from the source of life.

Because of sin (with the exception of the Virgin Mary), right from the time of birth, we are all brothers and sisters in this situation of rupture with God. And we all experience the tension and division between good and evil.

"So too with our minds: since they are animated by a holy natural inclination towards God, they have far more light in the intellect for seeing how worthy of love the godhead is than strength of will for loving it. Sin has weakened the human will far more than it has darkened the intellect."[5] We are all subjected to the struggles of our senses and passions which take us further away from God.

REDEEMED BY CHRIST

Saint Paul told us: "Therefore, just as sin came into the world through one man, and death came through sin, and so death spread to all because we have sinned" (Rom 5:12). But the love of God has torn us away from sin. God "took into consideration both the fact that Satan had caught the first man by surprise and the magnitude of the temptation that brought man to ruin. He saw that the entire human race was perishing by the fault of one single man. For these reasons he looked with pity upon our nature and resolved to have mercy upon it. But in order that his sweet mercy might be adorned with the beauty of his justice, he determined to save man by means of a strict redemption...."[6] God gave us the gift of his Son as our Redeemer and Savior.

Jesus, by his passion and death on the cross, showed us the wealth of his goodness, by obtaining for us a "redemption which is abundant, superabundant, magnificent and excessive."[7] In this way, "his mercy was more salutary to redeem the human race than Adam's misery was poisonous to ruin it."[8]

Let us contemplate about Christ in the mystery of his abasement: "who, though he was in the form of God, did not regard equality with God as something to be exploited, but emptied himself, taking the form of a slave, being born in human likeness. And being found in human form, he humbled himself and became obedient to the point of death—even death on a cross" (Phil 2:6–8). Christ totally adhered to the will of his Father who had chosen for him that he would live the mystery of suffering and death by making him a poor person amidst the poor. Jesus communed with human distress, he took on the destiny of the unhappy, and lived the drama of man, "as one from whom others hide their faces" (Isa 53:3).

In order to remove us from the misery of sin, God the Father modeled the Lord's traits on those of the poor people we all are. We are poor because of our condition as creatures; have we not received everything? We are poor above all because we carry within ourselves the misery of sin: "I do not understand my own actions. For I do not do what I want, but I do the very thing I hate" (Rom 7:14). Jesus, by the "yes" he gave to the will of his Father, reached the extreme in poverty, by assuming the destiny of a rejected man, sentenced to die, condemned to the most disgraceful punishment, the one on the cross. "Therefore God also highly exalted him and gave him the name that is above every name, so that at the name of Jesus every knee should bend, in heaven and on earth and under the earth, and every tongue should confess that Jesus Christ is Lord, to the glory of God the Father" (Phil 2:9–11).

Saved by Jesus Christ, we have to recognize him as the Lord, and therefore consider ourselves as poor. Like the blind man from Jericho begged Jesus to pity him, we must recognize our misery and call for help. We continuously need him to heal us so that he can free us from our sins. In him, we should draw from his well of strength to live out our condition of poverty, through the trials that affect us. Are we not tempted to withdraw into ourselves when we are afflicted with suffering, be it physical or moral? And when we advance in age and our capacities are diminished and when we must battle to keep a psychological equilibrium, let us join the Lord in his abasement. He told us: "Come to me, all you that are weary and carrying heavy burdens, and I will give you rest" (Mt 11:28).

Because we are redeemed by Christ, we must live as if we are resurrected, by sanctifying our trials and uniting them to the suffering of Christ, and by participating, through them, in the mission of his Church, which is the salvation of the world.

REFLECTION QUESTIONS

Do I recognize the common bond of salvation I share with my brothers and sisters in Christ? Our Lord has united all of us in his saving grace, and in a familial manner, as the Church, we comprise his Mystical Body, the Mystical Body of Christ. If it is needed, can I adjust my outlook and make room for this understanding of unity that I share with all of humanity?

DAY THREE

Called to Be Saints

FOCUS POINT

We are all—every one of us—called to be saints. Without exception, Jesus calls us to live our lives in him, to be strengthened by his grace, and made holy in his name. We are called to be saints, to go beyond our selfish boundaries, out into the world, sharing our love, Christ's love, with our brothers and sisters.

"True devotion does us no harm whatever, but instead perfects all things…. Care of one's family is rendered more peaceable, love of husband and wife more sincere, service to the State more faithful and every type of employment more pleasant and agreeable."[1]

On the day of our baptism, we went from death to life with Christ. The Spirit of love which unites the Father and Son had been spread into our hearts, making us children of God, disciples of the risen Christ. What that signifies is that God's will for us is our sanctification and that Christ repeats what he said to his disciples to us: "Be perfect, therefore, as your heavenly Father is perfect" (Mt 5:48).

This vocation to be saints addresses itself to each of us in a personal manner. We all must respond to it and personally commit ourselves to the path of sainthood. We do not have to carry this vocation out in an isolated fashion, but within the Church. Through baptism, we were made members of the Mystical Body of Christ. In fact, "the good will of God had been that man not receive sanctification and salvation separately, outside of all mutual connections; he wanted just the opposite, to make a people there who would know it in truth and serve it in sanctity."[2]

To live our baptism is to welcome our Lord's invitation to become saints. It is to accept to be a part of God's people in order to be sanctified in it. It is to open our hearts to his Spirit in order to be "made" children of God, day after day, and to participate in the mission of the Church which is to bring salvation to the world, through obedience to the Lord's own command: "Go therefore and make disciples of all nations, baptizing them in the name of the Father and of the Son and of the Holy Spirit, and teaching them to obey everything that I have commanded you" (Mt 28:19–20a).

The history of the Church is rich in teachings. Let us not be surprised to find a history of spirituality as well as one of its missions in it. Because of the sins within us, it is also, sadly, a history of the conflicts and tensions which have arisen in its midst. Let us know how to discover what is essential in it: the

Holy Spirit continually rejuvenates his Church and makes certain elite figures surge forth from it who renew its search for sanctity and rekindle its missionary dynamism. Saint Francis de Sales is one of these, one of those elite figures whose zeal reminds us that the vocation of sanctity is universal.

A VOCATION THAT ADDRESSES ITSELF TO EVERYONE WITHOUT EXCEPTION

No matter who we are, we are all called to be saints. "At the time of creation, God commanded plants to bring forth fruits, each one according to its kind (see Gen 1:1). In the same way, he commands Christians, the living plants of his Church, to bring forth the fruits of devotion, each according to his station and vocation.

"Devotion, the spiritual life, must be exercised in different ways by the gentleman, the worker, the soldier, the servant, the prince, the married woman, the widow or widower, and the young. Not only is this true, but the practice of devotion must also be adapted to the strength, temperament, activities, and duties of each person.

"Is it proper for a bishop to want to live a solitary life like a Carthusian? Or for a married man to want to own no property, like a Franciscan, for the skilled laborer to spend as much time in church as a Trappist, for a religious to be constantly at the service of his neighbor as a bishop is?

"Such a spiritual life would be preposterous, confusing, and, indeed, impossible."[3]

The path that leads to sanctity is not the same for everyone, but we are all invited to undertake the path. It is true that we are naturally lazy; there is a power of egoism and individualism within each of us that pushes us to keep to ourselves.

How often are we tempted to abandon any form of competition? Do we not live in a society that is marked by religious indifference, a characteristic of our era of scientific and technological progress? There is a risk that the will to be saints will dwindle within us, to the detriment of the Church, which has no use for our passivity and inertia.

TO BE SAINTS IN THE MIDST OF THE WORLD

This temptation to forget our vocation of sanctity is not something recent. During Saint Francis de Sales' life, in the 17th century, the idea prevailed that sanctity was reserved only for people who removed themselves from the world, entered into the religious life and shut themselves behind the cloisters of monasteries. However, "it is an error, if not heresy, to wish to banish the devout life from soldiers and sailors, mechanics and tradesmen, the statesman's office, or the home of married people. (...) Wherever we are, we can and should aspire to a perfect life."[4] This still remains true today. We must push aside all false pretexts of overwork or burnout and rediscover the true hierarchy of values. It is at the very heart of our life, in the midst of our activities that we must sanctify ourselves, not outside of our family or professional life, nor outside our leisure activities. To be saints is to blossom like Christ who steers us towards total success in our lives. We all have, at the very depth of our beings, an ardent thirst for happiness, a very firm will to succeed. Do we have any doubt that only Christ can steer us to this happiness, to this success? He is the Savior.

A BLOSSOMING SANCTITY

We have to experience the call to sanctity that the Lord addresses to us in the midst of the world, except when a particular vocation carries us to follow Christ, poor, chaste, and obedient. Don't be surprised if you are subjected to negative influences from our world. It is enough just to open your eyes: a whole way of thinking (in the prolongation of materialism and, more precisely, Marxism) imposes the condition on man that, in order for him to blossom, he must turn his back on God and reject religion, which is perceived as an opiate of the people. Without going into much detail, a good number of atheists estimate that the only people who could believe in God are those who don't believe in man. Even if so many men and women seem to live comfortably by having put God into parentheses, our world provides a sad spectacle of its ruptures, violence, and confrontations. The happiness of man could never come to be by forgetting God.

Let us deepen this marvel: Christ is the one who leads us to the full realization of ourselves. He is the way, the truth, and the life: it is he who leads us to the Father. To be searching for sanctity is not to be sad or to choose a bland life, it is to be on the path to happiness. It is to commit oneself to the happiness of others who are along our path. "The Holy Spirit assures us, through the words of our Lord and of all the saints that a devout life, above all things, is a life that is sweet, happy, and amiable. The world observes devout, spiritual people praying, fasting, enduring injuries, taking care of the sick, giving alms to the poor, keeping vigils, restraining anger, suppressing their illicit passions, giving up some sensual pleasures, and performing other deeds that may be rigorous or even painful to themselves. What the world cannot detect is the cordial inward devotion that renders all such actions joyful, agreeable, and easy."[5]

OPENING OURSELVES TO OTHERS

To deepen our vocation to be saints is to have confidence in God and make him the axis of our life. By opening ourselves to his love we are led, like Christ, to open ourselves to others. It is useful to ask ourselves these questions: What do we aim for in life? What gives meaning to our existence? What is our horizon?

Day after day, God wants to realize the work of our sanctification in us: "I am confident of this, that the one who began a good work among you will bring it to completion by the day of Jesus Christ" (Phil 1:6). Paul spoke from experience. Did he not accept losing everything in order to win Christ? And he became the apostle of all nations. Like him, let us allow ourselves to be loved by God and he will make us apostles for the world, effective men and women, committed to the construction of a more just and more fraternal world.

This takes courage, patience, and perseverance. Time and time again, we may have to start over hundreds of times. "Alas, it is sad to see some who perceive themselves still subject to imperfections after striving to be devout for a while and then begin to be discouraged and dissatisfied and subject to the temptation of giving up and going back to their old life. (…) We must not be disturbed by our imperfections, since for us perfection consists in fighting against them. We cannot fight them unless we see them, or overcome them unless we face them."[6]

An opening to God is an opening to others. The work of our sanctification is in a constant state of new beginnings. We are on the path to God who calls us. Day after day, we must make the effort to meet him through prayer and service to others.

REFLECTION QUESTIONS

Do I view each day as an opportunity to grow in my love for God, in my love for my brothers and sisters, in my desire to become a saint? Do I make it a point to pray for God's grace, to request that I be given the courage to love beyond my hesitation, beyond my fear, and enter into deeper union with our heavenly Father?

DAY FOUR

Union With God

FOCUS POINT

God beckons us at every turn; he longs to be with us; he loves to love us, and desires our love for him. There are many ways we can show God how much we love him, and deepen our union with him. And these ways need not be exceptional or dramatic. There are many "little kindnesses" we can give away to those around us: a smile, good humor, an open door, a few minutes to listen. God rejoices at our desire to be united with him through our love of our nieghbors.

"It is enough for me that God is God, his goodness infinite, and his perfection immense. Whether I die or whether I live matters little to me, since my dearly beloved lives eternally with an all-triumphant life. Death itself cannot afflict a heart that knows that its supreme love lives."[1]

B efore he knew the passion and the cross on Calvary, Christ said to his disciples: "I do not call you servants any longer, because the servant does not know what the master is doing; but I have called you friends, because I have made known to you everything that I have heard from my Father" (Jn 15:15). God speaks to our hearts in the work of our sanctification. It is he who takes the initiative. Just as he is the source of our existence, he is also the source of our sanctity. He is the one who frees us from sin and the one who gives us a share of his love all the way to eternal life.

To become saints means to allow ourselves to be captivated by God. He draws us to him through prayer. He comes to us through the sacraments. The essential component for sanctity is to live in an intimate relationship with God, to endlessly expand this union of heart he proposes to us. And if our heart allows itself to be radiated by the love of God, our life will become totally connected to his holy will. By allowing ourselves to be led by the Spirit of love that flows from the Holy Trinity, we will also always be more open to the requirements of the commandment of fraternal love; and the Lord will hire us for his vineyard. He will use us to build his kingdom. By following him, he will lead us to edify a more just and fraternal world.

The acceptance of our vocation to be saints does in no way mean that we are burdened with a back-breaking weight of rules and prohibitions. It is an acceptance to live in freedom, more exactly an acceptance to endlessly be free from sin, for a more complete gift to Christ. In the meantime, don't forget that this gift brings with it a rupture of egoism and it prolongs itself by our opening (ourselves) to others.

GOD'S KINDNESSES

We are saved by Christ, yet we continue to be subjected to the wranglings of sin. In order to motivate us to sanctity, "God's eternal love for us prepares our hearts by his inspiration so that we may love him."[2] "Our merciful Jesus, who has purchased us with his own blood, infinitely desires us to love him so that we may be saved forever, and he desires us to be saved so that we may love him forever. His love tends to our salvation, and our salvation tends to his love."[3] It is that God, "not only loved us before we were, but also to the end, that we might be and that we be holy. For this reason, by the blessings of his fatherly mercy, he prepares us and arouses our minds so as to move them to holy repentance and conversion."[4] The love of God the Creator doubles as a liberating love.

Because we abuse our freedom, we distance ourselves from God, and even turn away from him through sin. "In fact, we would rightly deserve to remain abandoned by God, since by this disloyalty we have thus forsaken him. But his eternal charity does not often permit his justice to impose such chastisement, but rather arouses his compassion and stirs him to rescue us from our misery. He does this by sending out the favoring wind of his most holy inspirations. It comes into our hearts with a gentle force; it seizes them and moves them; it lifts up out thoughts and thrusts our affections into the air of God's love."[5]

What will be our response to God's kindnesses? If we agree to open our hearts to his gifts, "if we do not reject the grace of holy love, it goes on expanding with continual increase in souls until they are entirely converted, just as mighty rivers coming upon open plains spread out and ever take up more space."[6]

What marvels of the infinite goodness of God! "Divine inspiration comes to us and comes to assist us beforehand,

and thus it stirs up our wills toward sacred love. If we do not reject it, it goes with us and enfolds us so as to arouse us and impel us ever forward more and more. If we do not abandon it, it does not abandon us until it has brought us into the harbor of most holy charity. For us it performs the three services that the great angel Raphael performed for his beloved Tobias. It guides us through our journey of holy penitence; it guards us from dangers and from the assaults of the devil, and it consoles, animates, and strengthens us in our difficulties."[7]

GOD IS THE GOD OF THE HUMAN HEART

Called to enter into the dynamic of love which God offers us, we rejoice to live in his presence. Saint Francis de Sales said that we delight in him in order to be marveled by his wealth and infinite perfections. One just has to take a look at young lovers, their behavior illustrates what the fervor of our response of love to God's call should be. "When we look at the very beautiful and natural love of two people, we see that the mind and the heart of the lover are always on the beloved. It occupies their time, their hearts, and their conversation. When the beloved is absent, how quickly they keep in touch through letters and all means of communication. The same is true for those who love God. You can never stop thinking about him, longing for him, aspiring toward him, and speaking about him."[8]

We delight in God, that is not only to live in an intimate relationship, it is also to savor his goodness, to "perfume" ourselves with all of his perfections. The soul in search of sanctity "feels the thrill and the thrust of incomparable joy arising from its pleasure as it beholds the treasures of perfection possessed by the king of its holy love. This holds above all when it sees that the king himself shows those treasures out of love and that among his perfections his infinite love shines brightly."[9]

GLORY AND PRAISE BE TO GOD

God's love is liberating; it prunes away so many of the useless desires which want to invade us so that we can search for the single, true good. Then these words of praise flow from our hearts; may the name of God "always be more and more blessed, exalted, praised, honored, and adored."[10]

But love goes even further. Beyond sentiments and words, it carries us to want good things from the beloved. The one who truly loves is full of kindnesses with regard to the beloved; he endlessly seeks to fulfill his beloved's wishes and desires. When we speak about God's love, we must admit our powerlessness. What could we wish for God that he doesn't already have in abundance? Is he not infinite perfection himself? In fact, "Since God is replete with goodness surpassing all praise and all honor, he receives neither advantage nor increase by all the benedictions we give him. Because of them he is neither richer nor greater and neither more contented nor happier. His happiness, his content, his grandeur, and his riches neither are nor can be anything else but his own divine, infinite goodness."[11]

If we can give God nothing that he doesn't already have, then we can offer him our praise and thanksgiving. And we can work so that the name of God is sanctified by the whole universe. "It is this divine passion that causes so many sermons to be preached, that enables the Xaviers, (...) the Anthonies, the throng of Jesuits, Capuchins, and other religious and ecclesiastics of every kind to endure so many perils in the

Indies, Japan, (…) in order to make known, acknowledged, and adored the sacred name of Jesus among those great nations. It is this holy passion which causes so many books of devotion to be written, so many churches, altars, and religious houses to be built. To conclude, it is this passion that makes so many of God's servants watch, labor, and die amid those flames of zeal which consume and devour them."[12]

In order to be authentic, the search for sanctity must spread itself into an intimate relationship with God which is always more intense. It must go even further and transform all of the existence of the one who accepts to be saved by Jesus Christ and led by his Spirit. If the name of God must be sanctified by the whole universe, it is also necessary that his will be done on earth as it is in heaven.

REFLECTION QUESTIONS

In what ways do I praise and glorify God? Can I set my outlook to the point at which every action on my part is done "for the greater glory of God"? Can I be conscious of every action on my part as being a means to praise and honor God's holy name?

DAY FIVE

To Do God's Will

FOCUS POINT

Adherence to God's will should blossom forth from our love for God. We so much love God that we desire to live our lives according to his will. This begins with us living our lives according to his commandments, and continues throughout our lives with regular prayer. We can discern God's holy will by remaining faithful to his holy word (Scripture) and communicating with him (prayer).

"Thus too, conformity of our heart with that of God is brought about when, by holy benevolence, we cast all our affections into the hands of his divine will so that they may be turned and directed as he chooses and shaped and formed according to his good pleasure. In this point consists the most profound obedience of love since it has no need to be roused up by threats or rewards or by any law or any commandment. It goes ahead

of all such things when it submits itself to God because of that unique most perfect goodness which is in him. Because of it, God merits that every will be obedient, subject, and submissive to him and that it be conformed and united forever everywhere, and in all things to his divine intentions."[1]

C ould we imagine clearer language? "Not everyone who says to me 'Lord, Lord,' will enter the kingdom of heaven, but only the one who does the will of my Father in heaven" (Mt 7:21). Without a doubt, the sanctity to which we are called brings us towards God with a love that we could qualify as affective, with a love that "fills us with pleasure, benevolence, and spiritual impulses, desires, aspirations, and fervors."[2] A soul that delights in God wants only to please God. It detaches itself from everything that could dissipate or turn it away from his sovereign goodness. God invites us to contemplate his beauty and perfections, to contemplate his providence and benevolence for his creatures. There is no sanctity without a heart to heart and an intimate relationship that grow together.

But the union with God must result in conformity to the good divine will. If I am pleased with God, I must also be pleasing to God. Saint Francis de Sales underlines, with emphasis, that affective love must prolong itself through effective love, the one that "pours into us the solid resolution, firm courage, and inviolable obedience required to carry out the ordinances of God's will, and to suffer, accept, approve, and embrace all that comes from his good pleasure."[3]

Because we delight in God through the marvels of his perfection and goodness, we submit ourselves to his holy will. And proof of the authenticity of our love for God is found in this adhesion to his holy will. Is it not through its fruits that we recognize the quality of the tree?

"TRUE DEVOTION"

Spiritual fervor and zeal for the kingdom of God led Francis de Sales to support a good number of generous souls seeking perfection and to write for their intentions. His "Introduction to the Devout Life"[4] had resounding success. The "devout life" (the words are somewhat outdated today) is not a question of sentimentality. It is the love for God with all its requirements, a love that gives us the strength to act and do good works "diligently, frequently, and readily."[5] It is affective love which becomes effective in order to realize all that we know to be agreeable to God and to generously fulfill all that appears to be his will. "By often taking delight in God we become conformed to God, and our will is transformed into that of his divine majesty by the pleasure it takes in him."[6]

This adhesion to the will of God is the fruit of love. It can only live in freedom. "Because this signified will of God proceeds by way of desire and not by way of absolute will, we can either follow it by obedience or resist it by disobedience. In this regard God makes three acts of will: he wills that we should be able to resist; he desires that we should not resist; and yet he allows us to resist if we so will. That we can resist depends on our natural state and liberty; that we do resist depends on our own malice; that we do not resist is according to the desire of divine goodness."[7]

WHERE IS GOD'S WILL?

Through his kindness and goodness, God communicates his will to us: "Christian doctrine clearly proposes to us the truths God wills us to believe, the goods he wills us to hope for, the punishments he wills us to fear, the things he wills us to love, the commandments he wills us to fulfill, and the counsels he desires us to follow. All this is called the signified will of God, because he has signified and made manifest his will and intention that all these things should be believed, hoped for, feared, loved, and practiced."[8]

Such is the general framework in which our search for sanctity must take place. But we must not forget that situations are concrete and the path to follow to grow in love for God may vary from one person to another. God's will for us also brings "particular commandments for each of us regarding our vocation."[9]

Are we not often tempted to see, in the different rules contained in the Word of God and in the teachings of the magisterium of the Church, as many prohibitions which impinge on our freedom of action and raise so many red flags which have no meaning for our times? Would we not have to free ourselves from so many "taboos," so many prohibitions that have "paralyzed" past generations? Today, let us all take notice of Saint Paul's warning: "So do not be foolish, but understand what the will of the Lord is" (Eph 5:17). Don't be hasty, let us constantly and humbly meditate on the Word of God which reveals the marvelous plan of the Father for humanity. Don't be hasty, always understand that Christ is the head of the Church and that he endlessly sanctifies it so that his salvation may be welcomed for the whole universe. Then, in faith and happiness, let us adhere to the will of God, to the moral rules of which the magisterium of the Church reminds us: they are in no way outdated for modern times.

Above all, may our adhesion to the will of God result from our love and not from fear. Obedience to the commandments of God and the Church cannot rest mainly on the fear of chastisement or the terror of hell. God asks an obedience through love from us, and an obedience that "has no need to be roused up by threats or rewards or by any law or commandment."[10]

"We must do everything through love and nothing by force; we must love obedience more than fear disobedience."[11] Love cannot be lived under constraint. It freely does all the beloved wants. That is why "the conformity of our heart with God's signified will consists in the fact that we want all that God's goodness signifies to us as his intention, so that we believe according to his teaching, hope according to his promises, fear according to his warnings, and love and live according to his ordinances and admonitions."[12]

God asks us to go even further through love; he told us "his good pleasure," and that through the events which are the expression of his divine providence in our regard. We must deal with daily realities through faith, with all the joys and sorrows they may bring. We must see the will of God for us there and "adore it as much when it sends us tribulations as when it sends us consolations."[13]

THE QUINTESSENCE OF SPIRITUAL LIFE

Through faith, we must abandon ourselves with confidence to the goodness of God. To adhere to the will of God even to the extent of the smallest of daily happenings is to discover his loving presence in everything. Let us look serenely upon all that happens to us, since we know that God is with us. And when the road is difficult, when the burden is heavy, let us keep peace in our hearts. "For, in everything and everywhere,

God loves those who, with a good heart and simply, in all occasions and circumstances, can say to him: your will be done."[14]

The union with God and conformity to the holy will of God are the two components of the search for perfection. On Good Friday, 1622, just a few months before his death, Francis de Sales expressed what we could consider to be his spiritual testament: "It is the quintessence of the spiritual life that perfect abandonment into the hands of the heavenly Father and this perfect indifference to that which is his will. (...) All the delays for our perfection come only from this default of abandonment; and it is true that we must start there, follow, and finish the spiritual life in the imitation of the Savior who did it with an admirable perfection at the beginning, during, and at the end of his life."[15]

REFLECTION QUESTIONS

In what ways do I discern God's will for my life? Am I faithful to the Ten Commandments? Do I practice spiritual reading on a regular basis? Do I pray regularly, expressing my thoughts and feelings to God in an effort to discern his will for my life?

DAY SIX

To Live in the Presence of God

FOCUS POINT

To live in the presence of God is to keep God in mind and heart all through the day, every day. Remaining in God's presence throughout the day calls us to reflect upon our thoughts and actions and how they relate to the reality of God in our lives and in our world. Living in the presence of God may even call us out of our daily routine, beckoning us to spend special periods of silence and solitude in God's loving presence.

"Remember to retire at various times into the deserts of your own heart even while outwardly engaged in discussions or engagements with others. The mental retreat cannot be penetrated by the people around you. They are standing around your body, not your heart. Your heart remains in the presence of God alone."[1]

At the heart of each baptized person, the Lord's Spirit is working. In the same movement it makes us recognize God as a Father and our neighbors as our brothers and sisters. It is not possible to be saints without living in the presence of God, without progressing in the intimate relationship he proposes to us, without being souls of prayer. That is the first condition of spiritual advancement.

THE FRUIT OF CONTEMPLATION

We are made in such a way that we are drawn by something good only if we recognize it and agree with it and it entices us. We must draw the assumption: the more we know God, the more we will also be drawn to him with an ardent desire to love him. The more we contemplate him, the more we also will be detached from earthly things, in order to only be drawn by him and attach ourselves to him alone. Our love for God could only be the fruit of contemplation: it could only result in the understanding of his grandeur and of the love he brings to us. That is the meaning of prayer: it allows us to meet God, to see his marvels and to meditate on them.

It is absolutely necessary for us to be souls of prayer. Saint Francis de Sales clearly gave us his reasons: "Prayer places our understanding in the brightness of God's light and exposes our will to the heat of his heavenly love. Thus nothing else more effectively purifies our understanding of its ignorance of our will of depraved affections than prayer. It is a river of life-giving water that makes the plants of our good desires grow green and flourish, and quenches the thirst of the passions within our hearts."[2]

There are many ways to pray. It is possible for us to use already made formulas which have been proposed to us. We can pray individually or in a group. Always, our prayer must be a meeting with the living God and an expression of our love. Francis de Sales' advice is always valid: "I put mental prayer (or prayer of the heart) in first place, particularly when it is centered on the life and passion of our Lord. By meditating on him frequently, your whole soul will be filled with him. Learn his ways and form your actions after his patterns. (…) Just as children learn speech from their parents, so by keeping close to our Savior in mediation and observing his words, deeds and affections we learn by his grace and example to speak, act, and will as he does."[3]

A CLOSENESS TO GOD

Whoever speaks of a life of prayer (whether it is spoken or mental) also speaks about times for prayer. Then an objection arises: we are overloaded with work, we have no or little time to pray. That is a hasty type of reasoning, a little like the hurried driver who, under the pretext of having a long way to go, wanted to avoid losing time and refused to stop for gas. A Christian should know to stop and pray. The time he could give to the Lord certainly depends upon his circumstances; above all on his greater or lesser faith and generosity. Let us respect our true priorities: "The time that we determine to give to God in prayer, let us give it to him with our free and unencumbered thoughts, with the resolution of never taking it back, no matter what happens to us, and keep this time for things which no longer belong to us."[4]

What is essential is to live constantly in the presence of God and to continuously grow in his closeness. "Recall, during the course of the day, as often as you can, the presence of God."[5] "Remember to retire at various times into the deserts of your own heart even while outwardly engaged in discussions or engagements with others. The mental retreat cannot be penetrated by the people around you. They are standing around your body, not your heart. Your heart remains in the presence of God alone."[6]

It is true, the rhythm of our life is considerably accelerated: the multiplicity of information which submerges us tends to make us forget what is essential, God. We must act to better perceive his love and allow ourselves to be drawn into the intimate relationship he proposes to us. Yes, it is possible to live in an intimate relationship with God, even in the midst of a very active existence. The dynamics and effectiveness of our work are in no way affected. This exercise of the presence of God throughout the day "may be interspersed throughout the day, in the middle of our activities. In this way our minds become used to intimate and private familiarity with God. Like one on a journey who pauses for refreshments, it does not hinder or delay the journey, but refreshes one for better traveling."[7]

CONNECTED TO REALITY

Authentic prayer, whether it is spoken or not, is contemplation on the marvels of God and an opening up in intimacy with the Lord. That in no way means that it is an evasion of reality, just the opposite. Prayer could never be a valid alibi for neglecting to respond to the requirements of our own vocations. If it is true prayer, it transforms our behaviors and gives them more conformity to those of Christ who we are contemplating. "Meditation properly then produces devout movements in the will, the affective part of the soul, such as love of God and neighbor, desire for heaven, zeal for souls, imitation of the life of Christ, compassion, awe, joy, and fear. It includes such actions as fear of God's displeasure, hell, and Judgment Day, confidence in God's mercy and goodness as well as deep sorrow for past sins."[8]

God wants to be with us so he can transform our presence to others. A true prayer is a prayer which betters the "quality" of our life, by giving free reign to the Holy Spirit who wants to free us from egoism and pride and make his fruit blossom within us: "The fruit of the Spirit is love, joy, peace, patience, kindness, generosity, faithfulness, gentleness, and self-control" (Gal 5:22–23).

Oftentimes we have little interest in prayer. That is because we have no need for conversion or because we have missed the target. We seek to feel emotions and find consolation in it. And when prayer becomes arduous, when we meet with spiritual aridity or dryness there, we are very quickly tempted to consider it to be a waste of time. Under the pretext of sincerity, we abandon it and fall into unfaithfulness. Isn't this very childish behavior? "Many men indeed take no delight in divine love unless it is candied over with the sugar of some sensual sweetness. They would willingly act like little children who, when someone gives them a piece of bread with honey on it, lick and suck out the honey and throw away the bread."[9]

God is always God; he deserves to be loved as much today when my prayer is arduous and seeded with difficulty, as when everything was fervent and a consolation. How many Christians have lost the meaning of prayer because they have lost the sensation of God's closeness? They will be lost in the clouds, totally strangers to what is happening around them in their lives. They think only of the existence of prayer in times of trial, when they need a certain favor or healing. Their prayer is no longer disinterested, it becomes a more or less magical incantation in order to avoid danger or gain an advantage.

For the Christian's prayer to be true it must then and above all be in praise of God. Simple or laborious, it must also conform our entire life to the holy will of the Father and impregnate all our behaviors with charity.

REFLECTION QUESTIONS

Do I contemplate upon the marvels and majesty of God? When I do think about the wonder and glory of God am I drawn to his presence? Do I make an effort to reflect during the day on the reality of my being in the presence of God at all times? Do I make an effort to pray consistently, even during those periods of aridity?

DAY SEVEN

Love for Your Neighbor

FOCUS POINT

We can be witnesses to the love of Christ. The opportunity to do this presents itself in myriad ways many times throughout our day. It is in imitation of Christ that we share in God's love for all his creation. We love God—we show God how much we love him—by acts of charity toward our brothers and sisters. Our day can be filled with "small kindnesses" in praise of God.

"Just as God created Man in his image and likeness, so also has he ordained for man a love in the image and likeness of the love due to his divinity…. For this reason the love of God not only often commands love of neighbor but it produces such love and even pours it into man's heart as its resemblance and image."[1]

In Greek philosophy, man is often defined as a rational animal; his grandeur is to be gifted with an intellect that is able to discern, with a will that is susceptible to making choices and to love. By greatly surpassing all animals, he can place himself before the infinite nature of God, perceive his love, and respond to it. Today, we are ill at ease with this vision of man which is too passive and leaves all of the riches of human relationships in the shadows. Another more dynamic vision has surged forth: man defines himself by his aims, by his relationships. The wealth of a personality is very connected to the quality of its presence to others.

Let us contemplate the mystery of the Incarnation. The Word was made flesh; it chose to become God-with-us. And its irruption into our existence constantly seasons our presence to others and puts into question the quality of that presence. To the Pharisee, who wanted to know what was the greatest commandment of the Law, Christ gave an unequivocal response: "You shall love the Lord your God with all your heart, and with all your soul, and with all your mind" (Mt 22:37). At the dawn of the third millennium, Christ gives the same answer to man who is thirsty for happiness and fulfillment. The testament he left with his friends before he went to join the Father brings us back to what is essential: "I give you a new commandment, that you love one another. Just as I have loved you, you also should love one another" (Jn 13:34).

THE SOURCE OF FRATERNAL CHARITY

The fraternal charity that the Lord demands of us is not the sentimental type, nor does it come from a natural inclination. It has its roots in a vision of faith: if our neighbor is our brother, it is because he is also a creature of God, a creature made in his image and likeness. "Why do we love ourselves in charity? Surely it is because we are God's image and likeness. Since all men have this same dignity, we also love them as ourselves, that is, in their character as most holy and living images of the divinity. It is in this character (...) that we are related to God by such a close alliance and such a loving dependence that nothing prevents him from saying that he is our Father, and from calling us his children."[2]

This mark of God which is etched into all humans is constantly thwarted by sin. No one escapes from the reactions of their beings of flesh when faced with others. Someone may appear sympathetic to us, another is antipathetic. Someone draws us to him today and seems seductive, yet tomorrow they may deeply irritate us. A certain behavior bothers us, yet another behavior enchants us. However, it is not possible for us to let ourselves, at the mercy of the waves which surge in our deep existence, to be drawn in. What is essential is elsewhere, it will steer our behaviors: "however, everything in us is the image of the Creator, we are consequently an image of each other, representing only a single same portrait which is God."[3] By reason of coming from the same source, "to love our neighbor in charity is to love God in man or man in God. It is to cherish God alone for love of himself and creatures for love of him."[4] What is astonishing then is that it would be necessary to have the strength of God to be able to obey the commandment he has given us. Love of our neighbor is born from the love of God as well as its source.

This love of neighbor finds its roots also in the mystery of the Redemption. The cross of Christ gathers us together into a single same family called the people of God, people who have been redeemed. Saint Francis de Sales shows us the result: "Saint Paul said love one another, like the Lord loved us. He offered himself as a sacrifice: what happened on the cross was that he spread his blood to the very last drop across the earth like a sacred cement with which he must and wants to cement, unite, join, and attach each and every stone of his Church to each other, who are his faithful, so that they will be so united that he will never find any division between them.... Oh how much this motive is pregnant to incite us to the love of this commandment and to its strict observance. We have also been sprayed with this precious blood, like a sacred cement, to bind and unite our hearts, one to the other!"[5]

Let us also not forget that we are all called to the Lord's supper which should produce the fruits of charity within our lives, in the Holy Spirit: "We are all the same body, we who partake of the only bread and the only chalice."[6]

PRACTICING CHARITY

Egoism is a tenacious traveling companion. It forces us to constantly put everything into question. It is so easy to content ourselves with nice words. Nevertheless, fraternal charity does not live by words alone, but in very concrete ways. "Love is patient; love is kind; love is not envious or boastful or arrogant or rude. It does not insist on its own way; it is not irritable or resentful; it does not rejoice in wrongdoing, but rejoices in the truth. It bears all things, believes all things, hopes all things, endures all things" (1 Cor 13:4–7).

To live the commandment is exacting because we must have the generosity and courage to accept others, just as they are, even with their faults. Love for our neighbor must be "a love that is firm, constant, invariable, which in no way attaches itself to foolishness, nor to people's qualities or circumstances, it is not subject either to change or aversions."[7] It is an imitation of our Lord who "supports us in our faults and imperfections, without either loving or favoring them; we must however do the same with respect to our brothers, never letting ourselves support these."[8]

Saint Francis de Sales added that the love of neighbor even makes us "condescend to the will of our neighbor,"[9] as long as it is not contrary to the will of God. It requires that we lucidly try to perceive what the impact of our behaviors is on those who travel the path with us. Without our knowledge, our way of doing things may be very disagreeable to others.

The practice of charity opens us to others who know difficulty and suffering. Francis de Sales wrote to one of his correspondents: "I counsel you to take the trouble to visit the hospitals from time to time, console the ill, consider their infirmities, soften your heart towards them and pray for them and help them."[10] Authentic love of neighbor will always push us to "procure as much good for him as possible, as much for the soul as for the body, by praying for him and serving him cordially as the situation presents itself."[11]

In the midst of the groups we are a part of (family, community, professional milieu), we must always make the effort to mutually support each other and go beyond the bumps in the road that may crop up. "We well know that our tempers flare into a million hatreds when someone attacks us and our self-love suggests that we always have bad feelings for those who attack us. But, by the grace of God, we can finally resist this urge, we don't let ourselves get caught up in this evil; at the least, if we are disturbed, we don't falter in any way."[12]

These hatreds are the expression of the sin within us which carries us to pass negative judgments on others. Are we not inclined to see the speck in our neighbor's eye without seeing the boulder that is in our own? In order to live in harmony and fraternity, is it not better to "always look favorably upon what we see our neighbor doing"?[13] Is it not more useful to "look at others' actions only to see virtues and not imperfections"?[14] Our social life is built one day at a time. It is better to adapt oneself to a positive outlook which validates others. Let us be aware of the garbage that provokes our critical spirit and negativity.

TO BE WITNESSES

The vast field of fraternal charity is the concrete ground where we should live out our search for sanctity. It is also the one where we can be better witnesses for Christ. We will be recognized as disciples of the risen Lord through the love that we have for each other. "However, if we want to show that we truly love God, and if we want others to believe us when we assure them of this, we had better love our brothers, serve them, and help them in their times of need."[15] It is impossible to cheat if someone says: "I love God and hates his brothers or sisters, (they) are liars; for those who do not love a brother or sister whom they have seen, cannot love God whom they have not seen" (1 Jn 4:20).

Divine blessings are acquired by the one who lets himself be led by the loving Spirit of the Lord: "God greatly favors those who practice charity towards their brothers and sisters; there is nothing that attracts his benevolence so much to us than that, so much that our Lord declared that it is his commandment that we cherish and love our neighbor; the same way that there is no greater love than the love of God."[16]

REFLECTION QUESTIONS

In what ways do I display my love for God through my service to my fellow brothers and sisters? Does my professed love for God translate into "small kindnesses" toward my brothers and sisters in Christ? In what new ways can I challenge myself to bear witness to God's love for his creation?

DAY EIGHT

The Lord's Eucharist

FOCUS POINT

It is in the Eucharist that Jesus Christ gives himself both to his Father as well as to every one of us. Jesus' great sacrifice unites mankind to God, healing a relationship previously fractured by original sin. It is this total giving and abandonment of self that we seek to imitate in our own lives, sharing the love of God with our brothers and sisters, and deepening our own relationship with Jesus in the process.

"In the 25 years that I served souls, my experience has made me aware of the all-powerful virtue of this divine Sacrament which strengthens their hearts in goodness, exempts them from evil, consoles them, and in a word, deifies them in this world, as long as they have sufficient faith, purity, and devotion."[1]

All baptized persons who allow themselves to be led by the Holy Spirit grow in the desire for perfection. The means to reach it vary according to the different stages of life. The path is not exactly the same for the religious as it is for married people. In every case, one must follow Christ, welcome his salvation, and dwell within him in order to live in his love. That is why the Lord's Eucharist could only be "the sun" of every Christian life, the sun which illuminates it and renders it productive. By speaking of the "most holy, sacred, and very sovereign Sacrifice of the Mass," Saint Francis de Sales defined it as "the center of our faith, the heart of our devotion, and the very soul of piety, the mystery in which God communicates himself and gloriously showers his gracious favors on us."[2]

A SACRIFICE WHERE CHRIST OFFERS HIMSELF FOR US

"Now before the festival of the Passover, Jesus knew that his hours had come to depart from this world and go to his Father. Having loved his own who were in the world, he loved them to the end" (Jn 13:1). It is not possible to understand the Eucharist without deepening the meaning of Holy Thursday. With his apostles, and for the last time, Jesus celebrated Passover. It was a ritualistic meal, rich in significance. Did he not remind the people of Israel of the power of Yahweh when he got them out of Egypt and freed them from slavery? Was it not a celebration of the parting of the Red Sea which opened the road to the Promised Land? In this last Passover, on the eve of Calvary, Jesus ate the paschal lamb with his loved ones. It was a memorial, through an act of thanksgiving, of the blood of the lamb that the Jews had spread long ago on the lintels of their doors so that the angel would pass them over without striking down their firstborn sons. This blood that saved was the celebration of the ancient covenant, sealed between Yahweh and his people which, generation after generation, the different sacrifices offered in the Temple in Jerusalem had consolidated.

But in the evening of Holy Thursday, this paschal meal was enriched with a new meaning. It proclaimed another immolation, another Passover (Easter), a new covenant, the one of the cross on Calvary, the one of the death and the Resurrection of the Savior. The institution of the Eucharist was the first act of Jesus' passion. Mysteriously and sacramentally, it was the anticipation of the redeeming sacrifice: "Then he took a loaf of bread, and when he had given thanks, he broke it and gave it to them, saying, 'This is my body, which is given for you. Do this in remembrance of me.' And he did the same with the cup after supper, saying, 'This cup that is poured out for you is the new covenant in my blood'" (Lk 22:19–20).

This first Eucharist, which occurred during a ritualistic meal, signified Christ's self-abandonment to the Father. When the time came for him to join the Father, he gave himself to him in a mysterious way, already manifesting the "yes" that he would give to his holy will in the Garden of Gethsemane, on the road to Calvary, and on the cross. It was the bloodless anticipation of the sacrifice which he would give to him by shedding his blood to the very last drop.

Celebrated at the very time when Jesus was going to leave his loved ones, this first Eucharist meant that he would not abandon them. Through this meal, he gathered them together in his love; that is why the betrayal had been revealed and Judas had left the group. He gathered them in unity by making himself become their nourishment under the appearance of bread and wine. Would he not also remind them of his single unique commandment ("This is my commandment, that you love one another as I have loved you"—Jn 15:12), not only in words but through an act; he washed the feet of his disciples.

The first Holy Thursday leads us to the true meaning of the Eucharist. Mass is the sacrifice where Christ offered himself to his Father for us. "It is very true that through the sacrifice of the cross, everything had been consumed and there was no longer any need for a new offering; however, it is no less true that the Eucharist is a sacrifice: there are not, in fact, two sacrifices, the one of the cross and the other of the altar, but only one, because, as for one as well as the other, it is the same thing that is offered, through the same sacrificer, to the same end, and to the same Father. For it is the same Christ who, for both, offers and is offered; it is the same heavenly Father to whom the offering is made, and that solely for the remission of sin and sanctification of the name of God."[3]

CHRIST'S SACRIFICE, OUR SACRIFICE

Christ offers himself to his Father at each Eucharist. Mass "is not so much a repetition of the offering made on the cross as its continuation and persevering reproduction, through which the redeeming Christ is offered and offers himself for all time to the Father, since the act of will is unique, perpetual, and very constant."[4] And when Christ said to his apostles: "Do this in remembrance of me," he gave himself to them as a holy victim so that they could offer this to the Father for the salvation of the world. Even if only the priest can repeat what the Lord did and consecrate the bread and wine to the body and blood of Christ, it is the entire eucharistic assembly which is invited to manifest this holy offering and offer this perfect victim to the

Father. "That is also why we, your servants, and your holy people with us, in remembrance of the blessed passion of your Son, Jesus Christ, our Lord, of his Resurrection, of his sojourn with the dead, and of his glorious ascension into heaven, we present you, God of glory and majesty, this offering which is a sample of the good things you have given us, the pure and holy sacrifice, the perfect sacrifice, the bread of eternal life, and the cup of salvation."[5]

Furthermore, Mass is our sacrifice in another particularly demanding way. Following Christ's example, we must unite ourselves to his offering and, to the Father, make the offering of ourselves, and of all that we are and all that makes up our lives. In this way, our entire life will be dedicated to the glory of God: "Through him, with him, in him, in the unity of the Holy Spirit, all glory and honor is yours, almighty Father, forever and ever."[6]

THE SACRAMENT WHERE CHRIST GIVES HIMSELF TO US

Throughout the entire time of his preaching, Christ prepared his disciples for the gift of his Eucharist. "Those who eat my flesh and drink my blood have eternal life, and I will raise them up on the last day" (Jn 6:54). These were intolerable words for certain disciples who left him. At every Mass, Jesus gives himself to us as nourishment under the appearance of bread and wine. We must recognize his presence through faith. We must welcome his salvation. An actualization of Christ's sacrifice realized in the time on Calvary, Mass offers us this salvation; but this salvation only becomes our own if we receive it through faith and if we welcome it as a reality that changes our existence and removes us from sin.

"Those who eat my flesh and drink my blood abide in me, and I in them" (Jn 6:56). Each Mass nourishes our intimate relationship with God; it consolidates the new covenant which helps us grow in the intimate relationship that the Holy Trinity proposes to us; it establishes us in the Church, since it unites us to each other in faithfulness to the commandment of love.

The Eucharist which opens us to God, opens us to our brothers. It must make manifest what Saint John the apostle said to us: "Christ laid down his life for us" (1 Jn 3:16). By receiving the risen Christ, we must become new people, arisen with him, that is to say, led by his spirit of love. By celebrating the mystery of Calvary, we are led by Christ to follow it, and make our attitude the same as his was, the one of the gift to the Father for the salvation of the world. Each time that we live the Eucharist, we welcome Christ, the bread broken for a new world. "I am the living bread that came down from heaven. Whoever eats of this bread will live forever; and the bread that I will give for the life of the world is my flesh" (Jn 6:51). If the Eucharist welds those people together, in love and unity, who participate in the same body, it does so to commit everyone, without exception, to build a new world, a world where mankind lives in filial relationships with the Father and, consequently, in fraternal relationships between themselves.

The Eucharist is truly the source of life if it transforms our daily existence and if it is given as an offering to the Father, through Christ and in the Holy Spirit, an offering realized in the faithfulness to the commandment of charity.

REFLECTION QUESTIONS

Do I recognize the transformation in my life when I receive the Eucharist? Does the "total giving" that is Jesus Christ make itself manifest in me? Do I seek to give myself away in service and love to those people I encounter throughout my day, seeking abandonment of selfish desire for the sake of closer love in Christ?

DAY NINE

To Grow in Humility

FOCUS POINT

The very root of the spiritual life is humility. The bitter pill of success can be difficult to swallow without humility. When the world defines success, it heaps the honor and glory upon an individual for *his* power, *his* talent, and *his* glory. But this perception is not based in reality. A humble heart recognizes that all his talent and success, every kindness he extends, comes from God, without whom one's very existence and capacity to love would not be.

"We must always hold firm in our two dear virtues, gentleness towards our neighbor and the very admirable humility towards God; and I hope that I will act in this way; because this great God who has taken you by the hand to draw you to him will not ever abandon you from the place where he has lodged you: 'in his eternal shelter' (see Ps 27:5). We must entirely re-

move all traces of pretense, since we only ever possess honor by scorning it...."[1]

L et us welcome the Lord's invitation to attend his school to learn from him what is gentle and humble in heart (see Mt 11:29). By being called to sanctity, we are invited to grow and to do it in humility. In the words of Saint Francis de Sales, this virtue of humility is "the basis and foundation of spiritual life,"[2] for it touches and attracts God's heart. "Humility is so necessary for us that without it, we can't be acceptable to God and we can have no other virtue, not even charity which brings perfection to everything, for it is so connected to humility that these two virtues can't be separated. Together, they both have such great empathy that one can't exist without the other. If you tell me that you have charity and that you don't have humility, I would reply that you are lying. If you assure (me) that you have humility and you don't have charity, you are saying nothing of any worth."[3]

Before being a way to act and behave with others, humility is a way of being before God, a way to situate ourselves in truth. It is for this reason that it is the basis and foundation of all perfection.

CREATURE OF GOD, MARKED BY SIN

Christian humility is etched into our condition as creatures. The word itself stems from "humus." That which is humble is lowly, close to the ground. The story of creation is woven into the Book of Genesis where God made himself life's craftsman, forming man from the dust of the ground, from the humus (see Gen 2:7). To be humble is then to be conscious of our creature condition, to accept that condition, with the resulting recognition and proclamation of God's grandeur: "Humble yourself before God. Know that the Lord is your God, and he made you; you have not made yourself. Oh God, I am the work of your hands."[4]

By reason of sin, it is not easy to accept our creature condition. Our pride brings with it a seed of rejection of God. It is a pretense of self-sufficiency, it is the refusal to be connected to the source of existence: "For my people have committed two evils: they have forsaken me, the fountain of living water, and dug cisterns for themselves, cracked cisterns that can hold no water" (Jer 2:13). We are all tempted to inflate ourselves with pride and we deserve to be questioned by Saint Paul: "What do you have that you did not receive? And if you received it, why do you boast as if it were not a gift?" (1 Cor 4:7).

It is true that our condition as sinners exacts humility from us, though it does not carry us directly to humiliation. We are redeemed sinners: Christ humbled himself in order to raise us up; he died on the cross in order to give us this divine life anew which we had rejected: "For our sake he made him to be sin who knew no sin, so that in him we might become the righteousness of God" (2 Cor 5:21). In humility, we must better perceive God's loving plan and welcome the salvation he offers us in Jesus Christ. Such a welcome does not happen without certain mistrust with respect to ourselves. We are freed from sin, yet we always suffer its consequences and oscillate between good and evil. But, as Francis said to us: "The mistrust that you have towards yourself is good if it will serve as the foundation of the trust that you must have in God."[5] Humility brings us closer to God, it open us to the immensity of his blessings. The smallness and greatness of man are for the greater glory of God.

A CONCERN FOR TRUTH

"Let us be what we are and let us be it well in order to honor the Master Worker who created us."[6] Francis de Sales' realism brings with it the necessity of truth, especially when he speaks about humility. Do we not all have a tendency to wear a mask and be devious, under the pretext of affirming our personality? To truly be humble, we must be true, not seek to delude or to cheat.

"Vainglory means the honor we assign to ourselves, whether for something that is not actually in us, or something in us but not of us, or something in us that is not really honorable. Noble ancestry, the patronage of powerful people, or material things are things that are not in us but rather in our ancestors or in the esteem of others. Some take pride in the possessions they have or the style of their clothes or in the amount of money they have. Could there be any greater folly than this?"[7] And to continue his great psychology: "Some like to be honored and respected by others because of a little bit of learning. Others have handsome physiques and therefore strut about to display it and spend untold hours to maintain it. Some brag about their prowess at athletics or dancing or games. All this is extremely vain and foolish, and the glory based on such a weak foundation is well called vain, foolish, and frivolous."[8]

Isn't it more important to remain simple, to exaggerate nothing, and to put everything into its rightful place? "Honors, dignities, and class prove themselves only under constant trial. It is not honor to be handsome if one prizes himself for it; if beauty is to have class it must be unstudied. Learning dishonors us when it inflates our minds and degenerates into mere pedantry. If we demand rank, place, or title, we simply demean them. Honor is an excellent thing when given to us freely, but it becomes base when demanded, sought after, or requested.

Flowers that are beautiful when grown in the earth, soon wither and fade when picked."[9]

But humility goes even further. It demands that we recognize our own weaknesses, it implies "true knowledge and voluntary recognition of our abjection."[10] Even better! We must not simply voluntarily recognize this abjection, but "love it and be gratified by it, not through a lack of courage or generosity, but to exalt the divine Majesty even more, and to greater esteem our neighbors in comparison to ourselves."[11] If we welcome the reality with all the humiliations that abjection carries with it, does abjection not exact this virtue of humility every day? "Some like to project the appearance of these virtues, but let the least sharp word be directed against them or the slightest injury be done to them and they show their arrogance. If we are proud, we let our feelings get hurt or are enraged by these slights, or even worse, our humility and meekness are artificial."[12]

WHERE THERE IS HUMILITY, THERE IS CHARITY

The human relationships that constitute the fiber of our existence are not sheltered from the strains of our pride and egoism. They are the vast field on which we must exercise humility. Do we not have double standards? "We like others to see what is good within ourselves, the qualities, positions, and duties to which we have been promoted, we want to be esteemed for them, although truly we are no worthier of esteem, nor greater before God; and, to the contrary, we want others to ignore our smallness and never look upon our misery, our faults, and imperfections."[13]

All human beings have the same value before God and

have been redeemed by the same blood of Christ. To be humble in the eyes of others is to respect the work of God in them. That necessitates that we go beyond appearances, not stop ourselves at the exterior (one person may impose himself on us, another may appear to be nothing), not let ourselves be seduced by that which is only an accessory, by wealth or social position. Under the spur of pride, we all feel the temptation to believe we are better and superior. We must fight to live in humility every day, without forgetting "that God resists the haughty and vainglorious and gives his grace to the humble."[14]

REFLECTION QUESTIONS

Am I aware of my lowliness, that without God, to whom goes all credit, glory, and honor, I would be nothing? Do I make it a habit to attribute all my blessings and talents to the great graciousness and generosity of God? If Jesus Christ, God in the flesh, lived in humility, who am I to take on airs, to believe I am of greater importance than others?

DAY TEN

Christian Happiness

FOCUS POINT

We belong to God. We are called by God, led by God in his grace, to be with him forever in heaven. Jesus has healed the wound of original sin to make this possible. It is difficult to be pessimistic about life when we consider how bright and hopeful is our future if we choose to journey with Jesus throughout our lives, always in the hope of the eternal peace of heaven.

"Keep your heart wide open before God; let us always be merry in his presence. This gentle Jesus loves us, cherishes us, and he is all ours; let us only be his, love him, and cherish him."[1]

"I don't know how I have been made; when I feel miserable, I don't trouble myself with it, and at times I am happy, thinking that I am truly a piece of work for the benevolence of God."[2]

W e must look at what God wants, and, knowing it, we must try to do it merrily, or at least courageously. (...) It's the goal of perfection to which we must all aim, and the one who gets closest to it will be the one who gets the prize."[3] In colorful language, Francis de Sales clearly defines the objective of Christian life: the search for divine will and its fulfillment in happiness and courage. "A sad saint is a sorry saint": the formula is not found in his writings, but is typical of his optimism and faith. "God is the God of happiness."[4]

OPTIMIST OR PESSIMIST?

We are beings of flesh with feelings and our more-or-less greater nervous resistance. We all have personal histories which belong only to us and contain the events that have profoundly touched us. We must admit that there are beings who are naturally inclined to optimism and others who constantly feel they are being led into the abyss of depression. The former always see the good side of things and their lives appear rosy. The latter have a tendency to see everything as black and constantly fight to find their equilibrium and fulfillment.

Without even speaking about the sick, whose bodies are affected, how many people suffer because their psyches are fragile? With the accelerated rhythm and invasion of technology that distances nature, these life conditions of our modern world do not make the task easy for them. We can't choose our crosses, and each of us must sanctify our own. This cross is often very heavy for those who are inclined to depression.

At this level of sensitivity and affectivity, optimism and pessimism are natural and have nothing to do with Christianity. That does not mean that faith has no role to play. It is the source of comfort and courage for those who put their personal difficulties into God's perspective and providence. Faith could even consolidate the defense systems of those who battle against their neurotic traits, waging a daily battle so as not to loose their footing. Their suffering is respectable. And faced with this suffering, the wide field of fraternal charity opens itself. We must know how to listen and let those who are depressed be heard and, thus, get help. We must accompany them without judging, without argument, without throwing ready-made solutions into their faces which have no effect on their torments. We must know how to be with them, by imitating Christ who wanted to be present to our misery. God-with-us.

A HAPPINESS THAT FLOWS FROM HOPE

The happiness that Christ offers us goes well beyond our sensitivity and affectivity. It is existential, since it gives meaning to our existence. "The mystery of man truly only comes to light through the mystery of the Incarnate Word."[5] Materialism has invaded our modern world, and for billions of human beings, death is the end of everything; they are victims of the loss of the meaning of God, carried away by the dizziness which shakes our times, in a search for well-being, more comfort, and more pleasure. In this world where the rich always want more and the poor always have less, more and more, man becomes his own devil. It is not surprising that this world is the stage for so much dejection and so many suicides!

We are God's creation, the work of a God who constantly wants to communicate his love to us. That is where the fundamental reason for our happiness is found. "We assert that God has had eternal and most perfect knowledge of the art of making the world for his own glory. Hence we say that in his divine intellect he arranges before everything else all the chief

parts of the universe which would render him glory, namely,
angelic nature and human nature. (…) Then in that same eternity, he provided and determined within himself all the means
needed by men and angels to attain the end for which he had
destined them."[6]

As creatures of God, we are filled with hope. Through his
fatherly love, he has manifested his mercy to us. He established that his Son "would redeem man not only by one of his
acts of love, which would have been more than sufficient to
ransom a thousand million worlds, but also by all those count-
less acts of love and those grievous sufferings which the Son
would perform and endure, to death, even to death on a cross,
to which he had destined him. Hence, he willed in this manner,
to make himself companion of our miseries so as afterwards
to make us companions of his glory."[7]

Even if we sin on a daily basis, God offers us his friend-
ship. Francis de Sales told us: "Keep your heart wide open
before God; let us always be merry in his presence."[8] Even if
we must constantly battle against our carnality which brings
us egoism, we know that we are loved by God and that he
wants us for his children. And that is the foundation of our
happiness. "What happiness, Madame, to be completely God's!
Because he loves his loved ones, he protects them, steers them
and puts them on the doorstep of the much-desired eternity.
Live in this manner, and never allow your soul to live in sad-
ness, bitterness of spirit, or be troubled, since the one who loved
it and died to give it life is so good, so gentle, and so loving."[9]

It is true that we remain beings destined to die. But we
have already been arisen by Christ who prepared a place for
us next to the Father. That is the hope which illuminates our
path and makes us strong in the face of trials which mark out
our existence. "We must have a simple sense of trust which

makes us live comfortably in the arms of our Father and our dear Mother, assured that our Lord and our Lady, like our dear Mother, will always protect us in her maternal way, since we are gathered here for her honor, and for the glory of her most cherished Son, who is our good Father and very gentle savior."[10]

SOWERS OF HAPPINESS

If Christian happiness has its roots in the multiple gifts of God, it is also a permanent conquest against egoism, with the strength of grace. "Rejoice in the Lord always; again I will say, rejoice. Let your gentleness be known to everyone. The Lord is near. Do not worry about anything, but in everything, by prayer and supplication with thanksgiving, let your requests be known to God. And the peace of God, which surpasses all understanding, will guard your hearts and minds in Christ Jesus" (Phil 4:4–7).

And the apostle Paul adds: "Finally, beloved, whatever is true, whatever is honorable, whatever is just, whatever is pure, whatever is pleasing, whatever is commendable, if there is any excellence and if there is anything worthy of praise, think about these things" (Phil 4:8). Christian happiness has nothing to do with passivity. The Lord mobilizes us, he wants to make us sowers of happiness. Let us be reminded of what he said to his apostles on the eve of his death: "I have said these things to you so that my joy may be in you, and that your joy may be complete. This is my commandment, that you love one another as I have loved you" (Jn 15:11–12). There is a such a close connection between happiness and fraternal charity: they are truly inseparable. One could even say that happiness flows from the gift of oneself. "Keep a spirit of holy happiness, which,

modestly spread across your actions and words, gives consolation to the good people who will see you, so that they glorify
God for it, that is our sole claim."[11]

It suffices to remember the beatitudes to be convinced of
this. We are disciples of a crucified Christ who gave his life for
the world and who leads us in his footsteps to give ourselves
to others. That cannot happen unless we die to ourselves, or
without a constant battle against egoism. The Spirit of love of
the Father and of the Son transforms our life and gives us true
happiness: "It is more blessed to give than to receive" (Acts
20:35).

REFLECTION QUESTIONS

Do I consider myself an optimist or a pessimist? Is there a
deep, abiding happiness that flows from the hope I have in
Jesus Christ? Does this happiness blossom and flow into my
daily life, moving me to serve others in a spirit of comradery
and joy? Am I filled with greater joy and hope the more I give
myself away, in imitation of Jesus Christ?

DAY ELEVEN

Fight for Faithfulness

FOCUS POINT

Through our faith history, even though mankind has at times turned its back on God, God has remained ever-faithful to his people. Our faith in God can waver at times, but we must never hesitate to call upon God's grace when our faith is in question. God's grace is generously given to his people. We can strengthen our own faith lives through acts of charity, and know God in a deeper way by sharing in and expressing his love for others.

"To live in truth and not in lies is to live a life that totally conforms to faith, bare and simple, according to the operations of grace, and not according to the operations of nature, because our imagination, senses, feelings, tastes, consolations, and conversations could be mistaken or erroneous."[1]

On the road to sanctity, the conditions differ for each of us but it is always necessary to follow Jesus, the one who is the path to the Father. Our condition as sinners makes us susceptible to deviate to the right or to the left. We must constantly fight to live in faithfulness. In the parable of the talents, the Lord distributed different gifts. But to each of his servants, he demanded them to esteem and propagate each of these gifts. And all of those who did this generously heard it said: "Well done, good and trustworthy slave; you have been trustworthy in a few things, I will put you in charge of many things; enter into the joy of your master" (Mt 25:21).

FAITH AS A RULE FOR LIFE

In the literal sense of the word, one who is faithful is one who lives in faith, who lets himself be led by faith and realizes its requirements. From the Latin word "fides" comes the English word "fidelity," which helps us perceive what faithfulness really means: to live all that faith demands. It is not simply to give an intellectual consent to the truths that God has revealed to us. It is necessary to truly risk everything on Christ. The person who is truly faithful is the one who attaches himself to him, through thick and thin, in all circumstances, and who acts in accordance with the gospel. Also, we can speak equally of the "Christians" or the "Faithful" in order to designate those who send themselves to the school of Jesus Christ.

Christian faithfulness has its roots in God's grace. It is his kind love which constantly renews us: through his inspirations, the Holy Spirit leads us so that our vocation to be children of the Father can blossom in trust and happiness.

The just live through faith. God's grace comes to help us in our misery; it frees us from the bonds of sin, and, by the sacrament of reconciliation, it starts us again back on the road of faithfulness. Like the Father of the prodigal child, God waits for us and offers us his kindnesses; in spite of our weaknesses and unfaithfulness, he celebrates our return.

GOD'S FAITHFULNESS

Our human language is very inadequate to describe the grandeur of God. God cannot act according to the truths he would have received elsewhere; he is truth himself. In this sense, we cannot speak of faithfulness in him; he is a sole and unique perfection, absolutely infinite. It is only within us that diversity is found; Saint Francis de Sales underlines it marvelously: "We have a wide diversity of faculties and habits. These too produce a wide variety of actions, and those actions an incomparable number of works. Thus the faculties of hearing, seeing, tasting, touching, moving, feeding, understanding, and willing differ from one another, as do the habits of speaking, walking, playing, singing, sewing, jumping, and swimming. So also the actions and works that issue from those faculties and habits differ greatly. It is not thus with God. In him there is only one most infinite perfection, and in that perfection only one sole most unique and most pure act."[2]

However, we must speak of God's faithfulness, the model for all faithfulness. There are no variations or weaknesses in him, not even the least inconstancy. He is good and faithful in his promises, and nothing, not even our ingratitude or our wickedness could alter his faithfulness. The entire history of salvation is an illustration of this. God has never strayed from his creative plan, nor has he from his salvation plan. In spite of the Deluge and Sodom and Gomorrah, God always remained faithful. And the old covenant, although so often jeered at by the people of God, had been replaced by the new covenant, the one that was sealed by the blood of his Son, who died on Calvary.

With insistence and constancy, God wants the people he has chosen to truly be his people. He removed them from all their infidelities, and, at times, punished them harshly, but it was always done so that they could return to him, to restore the covenant that he offered and which he has continued to offer since the first sin. God is faithful and he continuously calls us to come back to him, to be faithful to him.

A BATTLE FOR FAITHFULNESS

There is a profound inconstancy within us. Our sensitivity plays some very bad tricks on us. We are drawn by that which is pleasing to our senses. And even when we know what we must do, we don't always have the courage to do it. We are the "weak." We have our desires and aversions. And we often change our attitudes and moods which bring prejudice upon our spiritual life and to our progress towards sanctity.

"Were not our hearts burning within us while he was talking to us on the road, while he was opening the scriptures to us?" (Lk 24:32). The hearts of the disciples at Emmaus vibrated upon hearing the voice of the risen Savior. At times in prayer, we know this same warmth of God's presence. More often we experience no emotion and must continue in a state of aridity and spiritual dryness. It is difficult for us to accept such a situation, so difficult that we have the tendency to gauge the quality of our prayer according to the feelings we are experiencing. One day we want to pray; the next day, everything repulses us and we feel incapable of any prayer. We allow ourselves to be led by our feelings when we should be praying in faithfulness.

We must not let ourselves be discouraged. Even if we change, God never changes, and he always remains as gentle and merciful when we are weak and imperfect as when we are strong and perseverant. Let us not join the ranks of those who renounce prayer, under the pretext of authenticity and sincerity. We do not pray as a result of what we are experiencing, but to render glory to God and to express our love for him. "Today, you have consolation through prayer, you are encouraged and very resolved to serve God. But tomorrow, when you will be in a state of spiritual dryness, you will not feel like serving God. However, answer this, if you are governed by reason, don't you see that if it was good to serve God yesterday, it is also very good to serve him today and it will be very good to serve him tomorrow? For it is always the same God, as worthy to be loved when you are in spiritual dryness as when you are being consoled."[3] One thing is certain, progress in spiritual life requires constant effort in order to go beyond our variation in moods, so that we don't let ourselves be led by our feelings, but by faith.

Another great obstacle to our faithfulness is the temptation to escape ourselves by going into an imaginary world. There is no sanctity without adhesion to God's will which is also shown to us through the events which come to pass. We all have to sanctify the annoyances that happen in our daily lives. And still we believe that we can escape from this reality through dreams and imagination, by nourishing totally vain desires. "When we have certain duties and obligations, especially those pertaining to our vocations, it is a waste of time to long for and daydream about other walks of life. Why even wish for better gifts and talents to serve God better? Use the gifts that God has given you, because those are the ones he wants you to use. (…) If I desire the solitude of the Carthusians,

I am wasting my time and this desire takes the place of the one I should have to better use for my present vocation."[4]

Too often we do a balancing act between reality and the imaginary. How easy it is to be heroes and give everything to a noble cause in a dream! It is so easy because everything takes place in a world that doesn't exist. Christian perfection does not consist of being prodigies or submitting to martyrdom in our imaginations. It rests more simply in the acceptance of God's will, of his entire will, all the way to the littlest of things. "If any want to become my followers, let them deny themselves and take up their cross and follow me" (Mt 16:24). We are disciples of a crucified Christ, which means that we must have our feet on the ground, and that we must renounce living in the unreal in order to better sanctify the present reality.

In order to grow in faithfulness, we must also put into question our scale of values and rediscover what is essential. "It is not through the multiplicity of our works that we will please God, but by the love with which we do them."[5] It is the intensity of the charity which animates our prayer that gives it value; and not the facility with which we pray, and not the abundance of consolations we receive from it. It is the intensity of our love for God that we put into doing the littlest things that gives it value. "It is charity that gives value to our work."[6]

REFLECTION QUESTIONS

What are my feelings on my own faith life? At what times in my life do I feel that my faith is strongest? When things are going my way? Can I increase my acts of charity and nurture my prayer life in an effort to strengthen my faith for all occasions, whether they be happy times or periods of trial?

The Spirit of Renunciation and Freedom

FOCUS POINT

Habits can be positive or negative. Good habits can train us, helping us through trying times with a discipline that keeps us in a positive and healthy mind-set, ready to overcome any and all difficulties that come our way. These habits, or practices of renunciation and asceticism, can be gained through God's grace and our own willingness to practice them.

The best abjections (humiliations) "are those which we haven't chosen and which are the least agreeable, or, better stated, those for which we don't have much inclination, and speaking frankly, those of our vocation and profession."[1]

The most beautiful gardens require constant maintenance; if not, the weeds take over, stripping them of their beauty and compromising the quality and quantity of the harvest. In our interior garden, weeds also grow. They have very different and diverse names: egoism, pride, the search for the easy way out, envy, jealousy, laziness. Self-love can sum them all up. We must fight against them, weed them out so that they won't choke out the call to sanctity that the Lord repeats to us each day. It is a long and exacting fight which lasts our whole lifetime because these weeds are stubborn and tough. "Self-love only dies when we die, it has a thousand ways to entrench itself in our soul, and we do not know how to get rid of it. It is the eldest (of the problems) in our soul because it is natural, or at least co-natural. It has a legion of soldiers, movements, actions, and passions. It is adept and knows a thousand ways to twist and bend."[2]

Since self-love doesn't die when we are living, we must absolutely seek to control its effects. If we can't stop it from living, we can at least stop its reign. There is no sanctity without mortification, without constant and generous efforts to slow down everything which makes us concentrate on ourselves and pride within ourselves. "So if you have been raised with Christ, seek the things that are above, where Christ is, seated at the right hand of God. Set your minds on things that are above, not on things that are on earth, for you have died, and your life is hidden with Christ in God.... Put to death, therefore, whatever in you is earthly..." (Col 3:1–5). In order to follow the triumphant Christ on Easter morning, we must constantly die to sin and allow ourselves to be led by his Spirit of love. "Do you not know that in a race the runners all compete, but only one receives the prize? Run in such a way that you may win it. Athletes exercise self-control in all things; they do it to receive a perishable wreath, but we an imperishable one. So I do not run aimlessly, nor do I box as though beating the air; but I punish my body and enslave it, so that after proclaiming to others I myself should not be disqualified" (1 Cor 9:24–27).

SELF-CONTROL

Just as the athlete restricts himself to a rigorous lifestyle, Christians must conquer self-control. Mortification has a very precise objective: commit to the will of perfectly controlling the situation, to form the will so that it submits all movements of feelings, the whole world of passions, to the sovereignty of the love of God. Look at the comparison Saint Francis de Sales uses: "Ordinarily a wife changes her rank to that of her husband. She becomes a noblewoman if he is a nobleman, a queen if he is a king, a duchess if he is a duke. The will also changes in quality according to the love that it espouses. If the love is carnal, it is carnal; spiritual if the love is spiritual. So, too, like children born of a marriage of love with will, all the affections of desire, joy, hope, fear, and grief receive as a consequence their qualities from love."[3]

Within us, there is frequent tension between good and evil. Our will, instead of orienting everything in the direction of the will of God, lets itself be led by the things that seduce our senses. At times, the structure of our personality is compared to a great building whose lower floors comprise the world of tendencies, urges, with its unconscious part, the irrational and tyrannical. There is also the domain of sensuality, with all of its riches. There is above all intelligence and will that open us to the world of culture, art, and love which allow us to attain the love of God if we welcome his invitation to be his children.

Mortification does not have the objective of suppressing agitation of what we could call the inferior part of our soul. We will never eliminate the assaults of our sensuality, we will never quench the thirst for pleasure, riches, and power that is within us which so easily makes us forget what God's will for us is. Above all, it seeks to channel what exists into a positive vision of things, a power of life. It aims to consolidate the will which must govern the world of passions without allowing itself to be pulled this way and that, like a compass that would lose its true north. "Over this whole race of sexual appetites the will holds its empire; it rejects their solicitations, beats back their attacks, impedes their effects, and at the very least firmly refuses to give its consent. Without such consent they cannot harm us, and by refusal of it they remain vanquished, yes, in the long run laid low, weakened, worn-out, crushed, and if not completely dead, at least deadened or mortified."[4]

Don't make Christian mortification a simple technique of self-control. It is the search for the pure love of God. If the agitation of the inferior part of our soul must be dominated by the superior part, it is above all for the generous and total adhesion to the holy will of the Father. To mortify oneself, according to Saint Francis de Sales, is "to entirely leave our own will aside in order to spend our life in obedience and perfect submission" to the will of God, finally to offer him a heart "pure, clean, and emptied of our own will and self-love."[5]

MORTIFICATION OF THE HEART

With such a target, the best mortification is the one of the heart. "I could never approve the methods of those who try to reform a man by beginning with his exterior—his dress, his hair, his posture, and so on."[6] True mortification is interior which orients the totality of a life towards God. "Souls who desire for good and all to love God restrain their mind from thinking about worldly things so as to employ it more ardently in meditation on divine things, and they gather up all their efforts into their one sole intention of loving God alone. One who desires a thing but does not desire it because of God thereby desires God the less."[7]

This mortification of heart is renunciation, the spirit of sacrifice. It is a welcome to the will of God, so much so as it expresses itself throughout the events of each day, it is the generous and smiling acceptance of contrarieties which mark our route. This leads Saint Francis de Sales to say that the best mortifications will always be those which we have not chosen, on the condition that we put all our love into them: "The mortifications which are not a part of our own will are the best and most excellent ones, and also the ones we encounter along the road without thinking about them and those we do not seek, and daily ones even if they are small."[8] Daily reality inevitably associates us with the mystery of the cross.

We must not believe that exterior mortification is out-of-date. Control over passions requires that we know how to tame our body: it only comes through sacrifice. The stories of the saints are rich with impressive mortifications, often more admirable than deserving of imitation. It does in no means require that we put our health in danger, nor compromise our capacity to face our obligations. Let us not forget, meanwhile, that fasting has always had its place in the life of the Church, even today. It is true that the emphasis is a little displaced in order to better respond to the needs of our times: "Is not this the fast that I choose: to loose the bonds of injustice, to undo the thongs of the yoke, to let the oppressed go free, and to break every yoke? Is it not to share your bread with the hungry, and bring the homeless poor into your house; when you see the naked to cover them, and not to hide yourself from your own kin?" (Isa 58:6–7).

FREED FOR THE KINGDOM

The fast that pleases the Lord opens us to the suffering of others. Following Christ's example, mortification renders us free to better go to meet our brothers, to a better awareness of our place in the Church. It is only authentic when it makes our faith more active and able to better recognize Christ in the person of those who suffer the trial. A mortification that does not blossom in charity and which is accompanied by a shutting off of oneself quickly has the unpleasant smell of masochism and has nothing to do with Christianity.

"I am now rejoicing in my sufferings for your sake, and in my flesh I am completing what is lacking in Christ's afflictions for the sake of his body, that is, the Church" (Col 1:24). Just like Saint Paul, our trials and renunciation have value when they are united to the passion of Christ and offered to the Father for the salvation of the world. Following Christ who freely committed himself to the passion, let us also be free beings, called as we are to the freedom of the children of God.

REFLECTION QUESTIONS

Am I willing to practice acts of mortification for my own spiritual betterment? Am I willing to renounce those practices (or the excesses of certain practices) which do not bring me closer to God? When I do practice self-mortification (perhaps during Lent) do I feel more in touch with the suffering or hunger of my less fortunate brothers and sisters throughout the world?

DAY THIRTEEN

To Have the Soul of a Poor Person

FOCUS POINT

When we do not fill ourselves with material goods and selfish desires we open a space for loving and giving. The benefit to being poor in spirit is that one's life is not cluttered with "having," but rather is more concerned with sharing and giving what one has been given by God. It costs nothing to give another "small kindnesses." When we are poor in spirit we are more concerned with God than with what we can gain, possess, and control.

"Let us gently hide our smallness in the grandeur of God; and like a little chick who, all covered by his mother's wings, dwells in assurance and warmth, let us rest our hearts under the gentle and loving providence of our Lord, and shelter ourselves warmly under his holy protection."[1]

The first beatitude proclaimed by Christ on the mountain was the one of poverty: "Blessed are the poor in spirit, for theirs is the kingdom of heaven" (Mt 5:3). It was the first, not because it goes to the contrary of the most profound aspiration of the human being, who is constantly tempted to always want to possess even more. Christ offered it first because it is absolutely fundamental, and because it places us as creatures before the source of all goodness.

RECEIVE EVERYTHING FROM GOD

To be poor is to accept everything from God. Only he is the source of existence, only he is rich in mercy. In spite of our condition as sinners, he constantly offers us his love and tenderness. What makes us poor is that we are always on the side of those who receive. Saint Francis, by reminding us that we were created in the image and likeness of God, outlines the consequences of it: "In addition to this congruity based on likeness, there is an unparalleled correspondence between God and man because of their reciprocal perfection. This does not mean that God can receive any perfection from man. But just as man cannot be perfected except by the divine goodness, so also divine goodness can rightly exercise its perfection outside itself nowhere so well as upon our humanity. The one has great need and great capacity to receive good; the other has great abundance and great inclination to bestow it."[2] Better than all other images to illustrate this congruity of perfection is the example of the mother nursing her child: "Sometimes there are mothers with breasts so full and overflowing that they need to offer them to some other child. Although the child takes the breast with great avidity, the nursing mother gives it to him still more eagerly. The suckling child is urged on by its need, while the mother who gives him her milk is urged on by her own abundance."[3]

Blessed are those who, faced with God, place themselves in an attitude of openness and welcome. Evangelical poverty can only live in humility. The parable of the Pharisee and the tax collector shows this well. The Pharisee carries himself like a "rich man." He is rich in fasting, almsgiving, his perseverance in prayer, and his faithfulness to the Law. He is so rich that he encloses himself in an attitude of sufficiency. By doing this he cuts himself off from the source and closes himself to God. Also, he cannot be justified, since it is God alone who renders one just and gives salvation from sin. The tax collector (in the times of Christ, the tax collectors filled the tills of the occupying Romans and had the reputation of not forgetting their own personal interests) had the soul of a poor person; he proclaimed his smallness and misery, he abandoned himself, confident and joyous, to God who is rich in forgiveness. "I tell you, this man went down to his home justified rather than the other" (Lk 18:14).

OPEN TO OTHERS BECAUSE OF OUR POVERTY

It is not enough just to have the conviction that God is everything and that, without him, we are nothing. It is not enough to affirm that everything belongs to God and that, continually, we receive everything from him. Again, we must ensure that our relationships with others are impregnated with evangelical poverty.

When, in full health and strong, feeling sure of ourselves and about our capacities and initiatives, we feel superior to others, we are no longer poor people. Pride thrashes at us and exposes us to crush others to make them feel dependent upon us.

When we make ourselves the center of the world and act without concern for others, when we dispose of our free time and leisure without consideration for our entourage, we are not poor people; our egoism encloses us on ourselves, and we lose thousands of opportunities to give pleasure and bring happiness.

When we allow ourselves to fret through uncertainty about tomorrow and forget that God is the Father and everything comes from him; when we rebel in situations of lack of understanding, failure, solitude, when we accuse others in order to give an excuse for ourselves, we do not have an attitude of poverty.

When, in our life, in family and professional settings, we feel that we have been pushed aside, when we believe that the value of our qualities are not justly recognized, when we drop our arms and lack courage, we are not faithful to the poor Christ who knew humiliations and the abandonment of his loved ones.

And in our world of scientific progress which constantly lengthens our life expectancies, there comes a time when illness, invalidity, and aging renders us more and more dependent upon others, there's the temptation to lament and rebel at our lack of ability to act. All these miseries become poverty if we know how to join Christ in his destitution and suffering, if we know to suffer them for him in order to build his kingdom.

FACED WITH MATERIAL GOODS

Evangelical poverty demands that we also face material goods with an attitude of faith in providence, from which all good things come. It is a call for freedom, a call to rise above them, in order not to fall prisoner to material goods. Saint Francis de

Sales, by using the example of the halcyons, a type of mythical bird, marvelously stated: "Our Lord told us, 'Blessed are the poor in spirit, for theirs is the kingdom of heaven' (Mt 5:3). Cursed, then, are the rich in spirit, for the misery of hell is their lot. One is rich in spirit if his heart is set on riches, material wealth. Your heart must be open to heaven alone and impervious to wealth and all transitory things. No matter how much you possess, keep your heart free from the slightest attachment to them. Keep your mind and heart above them and while you may be surrounded by wealth, remain apart from them and master them. Do not allow the heavenly spirit to become captive to earthly goods. Remain superior to them and over them, not in them."[4]

There are many various and different personal situations because of different social and professional rankings. The gospel always calls us to a healthy realism; it asks us to live in the concrete situation by keeping perfect control of the desires which arise in us which make us want more than we need, and drive us to seek to hoard that which belongs to someone else. The fever of possession lurks over us all. "If you are strongly attached to the goods you possess, are too solicitous about them, set your heart on them, always have them in your thoughts and fear losing them with a strong, anxious fear, then you are subject to the fever of avarice."[5]

To those who enjoy wealth, Francis de Sales gives this advice: "Don't have a full and explicit desire for wealth you do not possess. Don't set your heart deeply in what you have. Don't grieve over losses you incur. Then you will have some grounds to believe that although rich in effect, you are not so in affection, but poor in spirit and consequently blessed because the kingdom of heaven belongs to you."[6]

But evangelical poverty also requires that we choose a

simple and poor lifestyle, even if we enjoy the benefits of the comforts of a condition of material goods or riches. There is no better indication of freedom with regard to riches than generosity and sharing with those in need. "Frequently give some of your property or goods to the poor, with a generous heart. To give away what we can afford, impoverishes ourselves in proportion to the gift. The more we give, the poorer we become. True, God will repay us not only in the next world but also in this. Nothing makes us so prosperous in this world as to give alms—such a rich and holy virtue!"[7]

It is not easy to live the beatitude of poverty in today's world. Social position is too often a function of the greatness of our revenues or the size of our fortunes. In this world that so easily loosens the meaning of God, let us make an effort to better practice fraternity and sharing, since we are all created in the image and likeness of God. And let us not forget what distinguishes us from animals. The difference between animals and man is with respect to their coats: animals' coats are connected to their flesh; those belonging to man are only added on in such a way that they can put them on or take them off when they want to. Poverty flows from faith, it is nourished by hope and blossoms in charity.

REFLECTION QUESTIONS

Am I open to the grace of God? Or am I cluttered with what I have, what I want, what I think I need in order to be happy? Do I deny myself those excesses which make me lax, causing me to forget the true spiritual nourishment I need to live in love and service to my brothers and sisters and to God?

DAY FOURTEEN
"Go Work in My Vineyard"

FOCUS POINT

We are all called to proclaim the word of God to everyone we encounter. We are, like the apostles, commissioned by Jesus Christ to spread the good news of salvation to the ends of the world, beginning in our own small corner of the world. God's love can be on display in our words and actions; our love for God and others can serve as the impetus for healing relationships between our brothers and sisters, bringing them and ourselves closer to God.

"After the love of our Lord, I recommend the one of his spouse, the Church.... Praise God a hundred times a day for being 'a daughter of the Church.'"[1]

"You also go into my vineyard, and I will pay you whatever is right (see Mt 20:4)...and we would say: firstly, that God had

destined a certain work to be done; secondly, that for this work,
he had prepared a payment; and, thirdly, that the payment will
be proportionate to the work done."[2]

W hen the prophet Isaiah announced the Messiah, he
revealed his name, Emmanuel, God-with-us. This "us"
contradicts an individualistic vision that tempts us all, God-
with-me. We are members of the people of God, which is no
longer just Israel but has broadened its dimension to include
all of humanity. The destiny of this people "is the kingdom of
God, inaugurated on earth by God himself, which will open
itself up again further until, at the end of time, it will finally
receive its fulfillment from God, when Christ, our life, will be
revealed (see Col 3:4) and 'the creation itself will be set free
from its bondage to decay and will obtain the freedom of the
glory of the children of God' (Rom 8:21)."[3] By our baptism,
we have become members of the Church.

This Church of Jesus Christ constantly receives, from its
head, the salvation which renders it holy and sanctifies each of
its members. It is also constantly sent out into the world to be
the sign and sacrament of salvation. "By obeying Christ's commandment, and motivated by the grace of the Holy Spirit and
charity, it becomes, by its actions, fully present to all men and
to all people, in order to bring them through the example set
by his life, through preaching, the sacraments and other means
of grace, to faith, freedom, and the peace of Christ, in such a
way that it is open to them as a free and sure pathway to the
full participation in Christ's mystery."[4]

APOSTLES OF JESUS CHRIST

It is not enough just to recognize that the Church has a mission of salvation in the world. We must also be conscious that this mission concerns us all, without exception. No matter who we are, we must take part in the missionary impetus which animates the people of God. And since the Church, led by the breath of the Holy Spirit that unites the Father and the Son, must follow the road that Christ followed to announce the good news to the poor, we too must accept to follow the same road, "the one of poverty, obedience, service, and sacrifice of self until death from which he rose triumphant through his Resurrection."[5]

There is great temptation for us to be disinterested in the mission of the Church and justify our passivity by thinking that the apostolate is something for priests and professionals who are hired by the Church. Such an attitude translates as a lack of faith. Our times are a good example of it, when religious indifference is a synonym for non-participation. We must hear anew the commandment that the Lord has given to each and every one of us: "Go work in my vineyard" (Mt 20:4).

A grasp of renewed consciousness of our responsibility to the mission of the Church is fundamental. Are we not each mutually supportive of one another within the people of God? "Indeed, the body does not consist of one member but of many. If the foot would say, 'Because I am not a hand, I do not belong to the body,' that would not make it any less a part of the body. And if the ear would say, 'Because I am not an eye, I do not belong to the body,' that would not make it any less a part of the body" (1 Cor 12:14–16). We all have a role to play in the Church.

In the history of the Church, Francis de Sales was a model of apostolic generosity. Saint Jeanne de Chantal affirmed: "in

my opinion, it seems that the zeal for the salvation of souls was
the dominant virtue of our blessed Father." Confronted with the
requirements of renewal which were proposed by the Council of
Trent, he committed himself with ardor in service to his diocese,
endlessly working to reform the methods of training its priests
and the spiritual life of its parishes. Today, it is not necessary for
us to copy his methods of ministry; above all, we must see how
great an apostle he was, notably by reason of the extraordinary
witness of sanctity he provided and that it irresistibly led those
who had witnessed it to follow Christ. He had profoundly renewed the interior life of a multitude of believers.

THE ZEAL FOR THE SALVATION OF SOULS

The missionary spirit which animates the Church, the zeal for
the salvation of souls, is the fruit of love: "Zeal is simply ardent love, or better, loving ardor."[6] The stronger our love for
God is, the stronger we are drawn "to hate, fly from, impede,
detest, reject, fight against, and beat down, if we can, all that
is contrary to God, that is, to his will, his glory, and the sanctification of his name."[7] This zeal has two dimensions: it tends
to shield the ones who perceive how much God is love from
everything that might lead them away from God; it strives to
lead those who don't perceive that God is love to him.

Born from love, the zeal to serve the Church and build the
kingdom implies a clear perception of the primacy of the love
of God and a deep faith. Jesus Christ alone is the Savior. We
are only useless servants whom he needs to bring his salvation
to the world. It is he who sends his most holy inspiration that
leads to faith; it is his Spirit who sanctifies. But he wants his
action of sanctification to be sustained by the quality of our
apostolic actions and by the generosity of our witness.

There is no authentic apostolate that is fruitful if it is not rooted in prayer and the spirit of sacrifice. If God is the one who fills us with his love, he is also the one who "nevertheless, wants to be begged, forced, and conquered by a type of obtrusiveness and diligent prayer."[8] And when Francis de Sales received his mission to go to Chablais to revive the Catholic faith of the region, he prepared himself for it "through fasting, vigils, mortifications, and continuous prayer."[9] To be a saint is to also be an apostle. The one who, led by the Holy Spirit, lets himself be carried towards the heights of God's love, opens himself to the mission of the Church, carries it in his prayer and generously commits himself to it as a function of his charisma. The one who gives of his person to the apostolate but does not make the effort to be connected to the source through prayer, dries up and falls prey to activism.

THE HOLY SPIRIT'S GIFTS

It is the same Holy Spirit who makes us saints and apostles for the Church and the world. He wants "to make our soul docile, tractable, and obedient to his divine movements and heavenly inspirations."[10] By his gifts, he allows each faithful person to "ascend from earth to heaven, to be united to the breast of God almighty and they will descend from heaven to earth to take their neighbor by the hand to lead him to heaven."[11]

In this movement of ascending to God, "fear makes us give up evil...piety arouses us to desire to do good...science enables us to know the good we must do and the evil we must flee...by fortitude, we take courage against all the difficulties in our enterprise...by counsel, we choose the means proper to do it...by intelligence, we unite our understanding to God so as to behold and penetrate the features of his infinite beauty...by wisdom, we join our will to God to savor and experience the sweetness of his incomprehensible goodness."[12]

From this union with God flows the "descent" to our neighbor to lead him to God. "The gift of wisdom fills our will with most ardent zeal and perfumes our soul with the perfumes of God's supreme charity...our gift of understanding receives an incomparable light and makes provision of the most excellent thoughts and maxims for the glory of God's beauty and goodness...by the gift of counsel, we consider by what means we may instill into our neighbor's minds the relish and esteem of God's sweetness...we gain courage and receive holy fortitude to overcome difficulties that may be met in this project...by the gift of knowledge, we begin to preach and exhort souls to follow virtue and to fly from vice...we strive to impress a holy fear upon them so that they may acknowledge God as their loving Father and obey him with filial fear...we urge them to fear God's judgments, so that by mingling such fear of damnation with filial reverence, they may more earnestly forsake earth to ascend to heaven with us."[13]

True devotion, according to Saint Francis de Sales, is meeting God, but also meeting mankind. It assumes the profile of Christ in order to build his kingdom for the glory of the Holy Trinity.

REFLECTION QUESTIONS

What steps do I take in my own life to "work in the vineyard"? Do I involve myself in parish programs that serve the poor and needy? Do I help to educate prospective members of the Church in their faith? Do I spread the good news of the gospel and the love of God to those people who need it the most, such as hospital patients, prisoners, or shut-ins?

DAY FIFTEEN

The Lord's Humble Servant

FOCUS POINT

"Thy will be done." The Blessed Virgin Mary is the shining example of humility and obedience. Like Mary, we must attempt to recognize our status as a creature of God, a servant of his will and grateful recipient of his loving care. A loving intercessor for all those who ask for her assistance, Mary rejoices in the humble heart and joyously commends our sincere prayers to God in heaven.

"Hail most gentle Virgin Mary, Mother of God. You are my Mother and my Queen; the reason I beg you to accept me as your son and servant is because I want no other Mother or Mistress than you. I pray to you, my good, gracious, and gentle Mother, then if it pleases you, console me in all my anguishes and tribulations, both spiritual and corporal."[1]

God chose to create us "to have company with his Son, to participate in his grace and glory, and to adore and praise him forevermore."[2] The Word was made flesh by making himself resemble us in everything except sin. Amongst all the women he could have chosen for the realization of this Incarnation, God chose "the most holy Virgin, our Lady, by means of whom the Savior of our souls would be not only man but also a child of the human race."[3] God's choice and this particular vocation gave the Virgin Mary a unique place in the life of the Church. It is a privileged place in the heart of each Christian who is marveled by the goodness of God.

THE MOST BELOVED OF ALL CREATURES

For nearly two thousand years, all generations have proclaimed praise for the Virgin Mary. Throughout his life, Francis de Sales had been in admiration of the Mother of God, the Mother of us all. She had been the object of God's kindnesses. By choosing her to be the Mother of the Savior, he had loved her with an absolutely incomparable love. Mary had been "raised to the highest distinction that there ever was and would ever be; for when it would please God to recreate many worlds a second time, however he could not make it so there would be a pure creature greater than the Mother of God."[4]

Called to a unique vocation, the Virgin had been prepared for her mission. To give birth, according to our human nature, to the one who would free us from sin, she had herself been totally saved and redeemed, in such a way that there would never be even the least sin in her. God "destined for his most holy Mother a favor worthy of the love of a Son who, since he is all-wise, all-powerful, and all-good, necessarily prepared a Mother in keeping with himself. Therefore, he willed that his redemption be applied to her in the form of a remedy that would keep her safe, so that the sin which spreads down from generation to generation would not reach her."[5] That is why "the torrent of original sin began to roll its fatal waves over the conception of this holy woman, with the same impetuous strength it had exerted at the conception of all Adam's other daughters,"[6] but it couldn't reach her; "original sin drew back its waters in reverence and awe at the presence of the true tabernacle of the eternal covenant."[7]

Filled with God, Mary benefitted from a "wondrous redemption, the masterpiece of our Redeemer and the first among all redemptions; by it the Son, with a true Son's heart, went beforehand to his Mother with blessings of sweetness and preserved her not only from sin, as were the angels, but even from all peril of sin and from all that could distract and retard her in the fulfillment of holy love."[8]

THE MOST LOVING OF ALL CREATURES

"The Mighty One has done great things for me, and holy is his name" (Lk 1:49). The Virgin Mary's loving response to God's gift is faultless. "She is the daughter of incomparable direction, the absolutely unique dove, the all-perfect spouse."[9]

Freed from all that could bring sin upon her, she was able to progress with no restrictions upon her loving response. "She never committed a venial sin, as the Church holds. Hence, for her there was no change or delay in her progress in love but by a perpetual advance she rose from love to love. She never experienced any conflict within the sensual appetite, and therefore, her love, like a true Solomon, reigned peaceably in her heart and performed all its acts at will."[10]

Everything else is our condition as sinners. We know the

strength of desire, the tyranny of our being of flesh. In us, there is a thirst for riches and possessions, accentuated by the advertisements that support these new desires and needs within us. We are also tortured by a powerful will; pride forces us to impose ourselves on others, belittling them and making them serve us. Day after day, we experience the tug of our instincts. The equilibrium of our lives is unstable; our faithfulness to the gospel, through chastity, poverty, humility, and openness to others, is a conquest that is constantly having to be re-begun. God's love experiences a thousand obstacles in us. Our spiritual life is a battle: "We see mighty rivers boil and leap up, roaring loudly in rugged narrows where rocks form shoals and reefs oppose and impede the water's flow; but on the contrary, on a plain, they roll along and flow smoothly and without effort. In like manner, the divine love encounters many obstacles and hindrances in men's souls—in fact, all have some, although in different degrees—then it does violence there, combats bad inclinations, strikes at the heart, pushes the will by different disturbances and various efforts to gain room for itself or at least to overcome such obstacles."[11]

Within Mary, everything is calm, peace and harmony. In her, love "is of itself sweet, gracious, peaceful, and tranquil."[12] "I say that in this heavenly Mother, all affections were so well arranged and ordered that love of God held empire and do-minion most peaceably without being troubled by diversity of wills and appetites or by contradiction of senses. Neither re-pugnance of natural appetites nor sensual movements ever went as far as sin, not even as far as venial sin. On the contrary, all was used holily and faithfully in the service of holy love."[13]

A marvel of grace, a marvel of the salvation of Jesus Christ, received through anticipation of plenitude! Everything in the Virgin Mary's existence was love, everything was a loving response to the blessings with which she was filled. Everything, even including her death. "It is impossible to imagine that she died any kind of death except that of love. It is the noblest of all deaths, and therefore the death due to the noblest life ever lived among creatures. It is the death of which the angels themselves would wish to die if they were subject to death."[14]

MARY, OUR MOTHER

The Virgin Mary was not just the mother of beautiful love, she is the mother of us all. Through her divine maternity, she didn't only give us the Savior, she actively participated in our salvation, sharing "all the pains, all the torments, troubles, sufferings, sorrows, and wounds, the passion, cross, and death itself of our Redeemer."[15] She entered entirely into the "yes" that her Son gave to the will of the Father. "Alas, the same nails that crucified the body of that divine Child also crucified the soul of his Mother. The same thorns that pierced his head, pierced through the soul of that all-sweet Mother. She felt the same miseries as her Son by commiseration, the same dolors by condolence, the same passion by compassion. In brief, the deadly sword that transpierced the body of that most beloved Son, pierced through the heart of that most loving Mother."[16]

At the foot of the cross, the Virgin Mary received us as her children. She burns with zeal for our salvation and intercedes for us poor sinners. Throughout her entire life, she led us to imitate her divine Son so as to steer us closer to him, into the kingdom. Let us contemplate her humility on the day of the Annunciation and discover that humility is not only a means for us to challenge ourselves, but a means for us to entrust ourselves to God. The Virgin, conscious of her unworthiness, trusted the Word of God. She was astonished at the angel's greeting, not because it announced the realization of the promise made to Israel, but because she had been chosen for the fulfillment of this promise.

Just like the Virgin, may we all always better contemplate God's marvels! May we all allow ourselves to be led, more and more, by the Holy Spirit who sanctifies: "Most holy Mother of God, incomparable vessel of election, queen of sovereign direction, you are the most lovable, the most loving, and the most beloved of all creatures. From all eternity, the heavenly Father's love found joy in you, and destined your chaste heart for the perfection of holy love, so that one day, you might love his only Son with a unique maternal love, even as he had loved him eternally with a unique paternal love."[17]

REFLECTION QUESTIONS

Do I call upon Mary's assistance when I am in need? Do I attempt to shape my obedience to God upon the model shown to the world in Mary? Can I commit myself to praying the rosary on a regular basis, asking the Blessed Virgin for her assistance in my becoming more humble in my relationship with Jesus?

Bibliography

Complete Works (Oeuvres complètes—referred to as OEA in footnotes), edited by the Sisters of the Visitation of Annecy, Niérat; Lyon, Paris, Vitte, 1892–1964, 26 volumes and 1 volume of tables.

Introduction to the Devout Life (by Saint Francis de Sales), edited and abridged by Msgr. Charles Dollen, Alba House Publishers: New York, 1992.

On the Love of God, Volumes 1 and 2 (by Saint Francis de Sales), translated by John K. Ryan, Image Books: Garden City, NY, 1963.

Spiritual Conversations (Entretiens Spirituels), (by Saint Francis de Sales), Pléiade, Gallimard: Paris, 1969.

Notes

INTRODUCTION

1. *Introduction to the Devout Life*, part two, chapter 14, p. 58. Please note that the following abbreviation is seen in the footnote citations: OEA, representing: *Complete Works* (Oeuvres complètes), edited by the Sisters of the Visitation of Annecy, Niérat; Lyon, Paris, Vitte, 1892–1964, 26 volumes and 1 volume of tables.

DAY ONE

1. *On the Love of God*, book 1, chapter 1, volume 1, p. 102.
2. Ibid, bk 2, chap 1, vol 1, p. 102.
3. Ibid, bk 2, chap 1, vol 1, p. 101–102.
4. Ibid, bk 2, chap 1, vol 1, p. 103.
5. Vatican Council II, *Gaudium et Spes*, 19 §1.
6. Op Cit, bk 2, chap 2, vol 1, p. 105–106.
7. Ibid, bk 2, chap 3, vol 1, p. 109.
8. *Introduction to the Devout Life*, part one, chapter 10, p. 18.

DAY TWO

1. *On the Love of God*, book 2, chapter 4, volume 1, p. 111.
2. Vatican Council II, *Gaudium et Spes*, 19 §1.
3. Op Cit, bk 2, chap 4, vol 1, p. 111.
4. Ibid, bk 2, chap 4, vol 1, p. 111–112.
5. Ibid, bk 1, chap 17, vol 1, p. 95.
6. Ibid, bk 2, chap 4, vol 1, p. 113.
7. Ibid, bk 2, chap 4, vol 1, p. 113.
8. Ibid, bk 2, chap 5, vol 1, p. 115.

DAY THREE

1. *Introduction to the Devout Life*, part one, chapter 3, p. 8.
2. Vatican Council II, *Lumen Gentium*, no. 9.
3. Op Cit, part one, chap 3, p. 7.
4. Ibid, part one, chap 3, p. 8.
5. Ibid, part one, chap 2, p. 5.
6. Ibid, part one, chap 5, p. 11.

DAY FOUR

1. *On the Love of God*, book 5, chapter 3, volume 1, p. 243.
2. Ibid, bk 2, title of chap 9, vol 1, p. 123.
3. Ibid, bk 2, chap 8, vol 1, p. 121.
4. Ibid, bk 2, chap 9, vol 1, p. 125.
5. Ibid, bk 2, chap 9, vol 1, p. 125.
6. Ibid, bk 2, chap 21, vol 1, p. 159.
7. Ibid, bk 2, chap 21, vol 1, p. 160.
8. *Introduction to the Devout Life*, part two, chapter 13, p. 57.
9. Op Cit, bk 5, chap 2, vol 1, p. 237.
10. Ibid, bk 5, chap 8, vol 1, p. 254.
11. Ibid, bk 5, chap 8, vol 1, p. 253.
12. Ibid, bk 5, chap 9, vol 1, p. 258.

DAY FIVE

1. *On the Love of God*, book 8, chapter 2, volume 2, p. 61.
2. Ibid, bk 6, chap 1, vol 1, p. 267.
3. Ibid, bk 6, chap 1, vol 1, p. 267.
4. Published in 1608 in Lyon (France)
5. *Introduction to the Devout Life*, part one, chapter 1, p. 4.
6. *On the Love of God*, book 8, chapter 1, volume 2, p. 58.
7. Ibid, bk 8, chap 3, vol 2, p. 62.
8. Ibid, bk 8, chap 3, vol 2, p. 62.
9. OEA, vol XII, p. 347: Letters to President Brulart, October 13, 1604.
10. Op Cit, bk 8, chap 2, vol 2, p. 61.
11. OEA, vol XII, p. 359: Letter to Baroness de Chantal, October 14, 1604.
12. Op Cit, bk 8, chap 3, vol 2, p. 63.
13. OEA, vol XXI, p. 18: Letter to a Lady, no date.
14. OEA, vol XIV, p. 75: Letter to Miss Clément, October, 1608.
15. OEA, vol X, p. 389: Sermon for Good Friday.

DAY SIX

1. *Introduction to the Devout Life*, part two, chapter 12, p. 55.
2. Ibid, part two, chap 1, p. 43.
3. Ibid, part two, chap 1, p. 43.
4. OEA, vol XIV, p. 103: Letter to the Baroness de Chantal, no date.
5. Op Cit, part two, chap 12, p. 55.
6. Ibid, part two, chap 12, p. 55.
7. Ibid, part two, chap 13, p. 56.
8. Ibid, part two, chap 6, p. 49.
9. *On the Love of God*, book 9, chapter 10, volume 2, p. 123.

DAY SEVEN

1. *On the Love of God*, book 10, chapter 11, volume 2, p. 170, 172.
2. Ibid, bk 10, chap 11, vol 2, p. 171.
3. OEA, vol X, p. 270: Sermon for the third Sunday of Lent.
4. Op Cit, bk 10, chap 11, vol 2, p. 171.
5. OEA, vol X, p. 277–278: Sermon for the third Sunday of Lent.
6. Ibid, vol VIII, p. 13: Sermon about holy Communion.
7. Ibid, vol IX, p. 200: Sermon for the seventeenth Sunday after Pentecost.
8. Ibid, p. 200–201.
9. Ibid, vol XII, p. 270: Letter to President Brulart, May 3, 1604.
10. Ibid, p. 270.
11. Conversations (about cordiality), p. 117.
12. OEA, vol XVI, p. 222: Letter to Madame de la Fléchère, August–September, 1614.
13. Conversations (on the spirit of humility), p. 1120.
14. Ibid, p. 1606.
15. OEA, vol X, p. 65: Sermon for the feast of the Visitation.
16. Ibid, vol X, p. 235: Sermon for the second Sunday of Lent.

DAY EIGHT

1. OEA, vol XVI, p. 57–58: Letter to the Duke of Bellegarde, August 24, 1613.
2. *Introduction to the Devout Life*, part two, chapter 14, p. 58.
3. OEA, vol XXIII, p. 103: Pamphlets.
4. Ibid, p. 104.
5. First Eucharistic Prayer.
6. Conclusion of the Eucharistic Prayer.

DAY NINE

1. OEA, vol XVIII, p. 135: Letter to Madame de la Valbonne around 1617.
2. Ibid, vol IX, p. 163: Sermon for the feast of the Visitation.
3. Ibid, vol IX, p. 224–225: Sermon for the feast of SS. Cosmas and Damian.
4. *Introduction to the Devout Life,* part one, chapter 9, p. 17.
5. OEA, vol XVII, p. 259: Letter to Mother de Bréchard, July 22, 1616.
6. Ibid, vol XIII, p. 53–54: Letter to President Brulart, June 10, 1605.
7. *Introduction to the Devout Life,* part three, chapter 4, p. 81.
8. Ibid, p. 81.
9. Ibid, p. 82.
10. Ibid, part three, chap 6, p. 86.
11. Ibid, p. 87.
12. Ibid, part three, chap 8, p. 90.
13. OEA, vol IX, p. 108: Sermon for the feast of Saint Michael the Archangel.
14. Ibid, vol XVIII, p. 129: Letter to Madame de Chailliol, December 27, 1617.

DAY TEN

1. OEA, vol. XIII, p. 193: Letter to the Baroness de Chantal, June 17, 1606.
2. Ibid, p. 366: Letter to the Baroness de Chantal, March 4, 1608.
3. Ibid, p. 20–21: Letter to President Brulart, March, 1605.
4. Ibid, p. 16: Letter to President Brulart, February, 1605.
5. Second Vatican Council, *Gaudium et Spes,* no. 22 §1.
6. *On the Love of God,* book 2, chapter 3, volume 1, p. 108.
7. Ibid, bk 2, chap 4, vol 1, p. 113.
8. OEA, vol XIII, p. 193: Letter to the Baroness de Chantal, June 17, 1606.
9. Ibid, vol XVIII, p. 59: Letter to a Lady, August 7, 1617.
10. Conversations (about simplicity), p. 1197–1198.
11. Op Cit, vol XIV, p. 57: Letter to Madame de la Fléchère, August, 1608.

DAY ELEVEN

1. OEA, Vol XX, p. 194: Letter to Sister de Blonay, November 28, 1621.
2. *On the Love of God*, book 2, chapter 2, volume 1, p. 103–104.
3. OEA, vol VI, p. 36: About Firmness.
4. *Introduction to the Devout Life*, part three, chapter 37, p. 133.
5. Conversations (last conversations), p. 1307.
6. Ibid, p. 1308.

DAY TWELVE

1. OEA, vol XIII, p. 206: Letter to the Baroness de Chantal, August 6, 1606.
2. Ibid, vol XII, p. 383: Letter to the Baroness de Chantal.
3. *On the Love of God*, book 1, chapter 4, volume 1, p. 61.
4. Ibid, bk 1, chap 3, vol 1, p. 59.
5. OEA, vol IX, p. 106: Sermon for the feast of Saint Michael the Archangel.
6. *Introduction to the Devout Life*, part three, chapter 23, p. 114.
7. *On the Love of God*, book 12, chapter 3, volume 2, p. 264–265.
8. Conversations, p. 1326 (Appendix).

DAY THIRTEEN

1. OEA, vol XX, p. 134: Letter to Mother de Chantal, August 24, 1621.
2. *On the Love of God*, book 1, chapter 15, volume 1, p. 91.
3. Ibid, p. 92.
4. *Introduction to the Devout Life*, part three, chapter 14, p. 99–100.
5. Ibid, p. 100.
6. Ibid, p. 101.
7. Ibid, part three, chap 15, p. 102.

DAY FOURTEEN

1. OEA, vol XII, p. 266: Letter to the Baroness de Chantal, May 3, 1604.
2. Ibid, vol VIII, p. 391–392: Sermon for Septuagesima Sunday.
3. Vatican Council II, *Lumen Gentium*, no. 9.

4. Ibid, *Ad Gentes*, no. 5.
5. Ibid, no. 5.
6. *On the Love of God*, book 10, chapter 12, volume 2, p. 173.
7. Ibid, bk 10, chap 14, vol 2, p. 179.
8. OEA, vol XXIV, p. 342: Pamphlets.
9. Ibid.
10. *On the Love of God*, book 11, chapter 15, volume 2, p. 240.
11. Ibid, p. 240.
12. Ibid, p. 240–241.
13. Ibid, p. 241.

DAY FIFTEEN

1. OEA, vol XXVI, p. 429, Prayer to the Blessed Virgin attributed to Saint Francis de Sales.
2. *On the Love of God*, book 2, chapter 4, volume 1, p. 112.
3. Ibid, p. 112.
4. OEA, vol X, p. 53: Sermon for the feast of the Annunciation.
5. Op Cit, bk 2, chap 6, vol 1, p. 116.
6. Ibid, p. 116.
7. Ibid, p. 117.
8. Ibid, p. 117.
9. Ibid, bk 3, chap 8, vol 1, p. 182.
10. Ibid, p. 183.
11. Ibid, bk 7, chap 14, vol 2, p. 52.
12. Ibid, p. 52.
13. Ibid, p. 53.
14. Ibid, p. 49.
15. Ibid, bk 5, chap 4, vol 1, p. 243–244.
16. Ibid, p. 244.
17. Ibid, volume 1, Dedicatory Prayer, p. 34.